I Ching

BANTAM BOOKS

New York · Toronto · London · Sydney · Auckland

I Ching

A New Interpretation

For Modern Times

Sam Reifler

Oracles rephrased as poetry

with the help of Alan Ravage

I CHING

A Bantam Book

Bantam rack edition / March 1974

Bantam Trade Paperback edition / December 1991

Bantam New Age and the accompanying figure design as well as "the search for meaning, growth and change" are trademarks of Bantam Books, a division of Bantam Doubleday Dell Publishing Group, Inc.

Library of Congress Cataloging-in-Publication Data
Reifler, Sam.
I ching: a new interpretation for modern times / Sam Reifler :
oracles rephrased as poetry with the help of Alan Ravage. — Bantam
trade pbk. ed.
p.   cm.
ISBN 0-553-35424-8
1. I ching.   I. Title.
PL2478.D67   1991
299'.51282—dc20   *91-9870*
                                                              CIP

Published simultaneously in the United States and Canada

PRINTED IN THE UNITED STATES OF AMERICA

20 19 18 17 16 15 14 13 12

Table of Contents

Contents

Introduction

Like its Western counterparts, such as astrology and tarot reading, the I Ching is most often used as a parlor game. Such parlor games are faddish popular offsprings of a genuine spiritual revival movement. This resurgence of spiritual exploration is hardly the most original aspect of the new culture. Its forerunner can be found at the turn of the century, when Yeats and Conan Doyle were seriously immersed in spiritualism, when even Boston's stodgy James brothers and pukka Kipling dabbled in it, when séances were held in the White House, and when the names of magicians, fortune-tellers and mediums, such as D. D. Home, Eusapia Paladino and the Poughkeepsie Twins were household terms. At the turn of the century there were at least as many Ouija boards and tarot decks and tapping tables among female college students as there are now. (There were few I Chings, if any, however.) The wellspring of that former spiritual revival was spiritualism: the belief that a spirit continues to exist after the death of the body. Its sources were mainly Celtic and continental Christian heresies of magic and witchcraft. An inner sanctum interest in Hinduism revolved around *amatman*, its concept of reincarnation. Do souls transmigrate? It was a moot question for some people. For most it was parlor talk that went with parlor games.

Our present spiritual revival was touched off by an idea from the East, so unlike Victorian-style spiritualism that they can hardly be compared: the Buddhist way of acceptance, of being part of all existence, without posing values and making judgments. The Beat Generation picked it up from its early American discoverers, Alan Watts, Gary Snyder, Thomas Merton, etc., and published it, and it has permeated the culture and can be found in a perverted form in political dialectic and television commercials. This idea enables one to perceive a basic unity among all things— all things that are the Whole, the All, the One: the Ineffable. (As soon as "it" is named, "it" is limited and, therefore, "it" is not It anymore. The Zen master felt that he could only point at "it," not name "it.") The Taoists of ancient China, formulators of the I Ching, called it Tao, the Way. The experience of this idea has developed in the new generation a more neutral, less ambitious and less neurotic attitude toward the material world. It has also made the Victorian problems of spiritualism irrelevant, because Life and Death, as well as Time, are now regarded as nothing more than cultural concepts: karma, maya, excess baggage on our perpetual way in and out of the present moment.

Concurrent with the West Coast's discovery of Zen in the 1950s was the beginning of the present burgeoning use and acceptance of drugs. Jazz musicians gifted poet friends with marijuana and western-states intellectuals experimented with the Indian's magic mushroom mescaline. These drugs, in Huxley's phrase, "opened the doors of perception."

Buddha says Form is Void. If we could live for a few moments without any discrimination whatsoever, without discriminating relative densities, without discriminating colors, without discriminating by focusing or concentrating on particular frequencies or pitches of sound, etc.—we would be nowhere, in a void, nothing. Everything we experience we have been taught to experience—from the basic operation of the senses to the perception of complicated systems changing rapidly in time. The same is true for all we believe and all we know, from the concept of a somewhat spheroid-shaped planet to the concept that theft and vandalism are unethical. One should not gloss over the importance of the drug subculture to the spiritual revival and moral reorganization taking place in the culture as a whole. The religious/philosophical revelations of the progenitors of the present spiritual revival went hand in hand with the consciousness-expanding effects of their drugs, which freed them to perceive patterns in the void other than those generally recognized within the culture. At first these revelations were within a strictly personal framework as the drug pioneers moved outside the confines of the old culture without yet being part of a new culture. As the use of drugs became more widespread certain meaningful patterns within the Western culture, lately buried by the materialistic scientific bonanza of our times, and meaningful patterns from other cultures, began to emerge. These once exotic and esoteric ideas are gradually taking their place as meaningful concepts in the American culture as a whole: priests have rediscovered Christ; middle-aged housewives study yoga at the YWCA; computerized astrology is respectable and profitable; the wealthiest, most powerful class buy LSD therapy in a London clinic; young psychiatrists have begun again to sense the divinity of the madman; and bronze Chinese coins rattle nightly on kitchen tables from coast to coast. The coins are thrown eagerly, swiftly; bystanders comment on the lines of the forming hexagrams; there is a general discussion on interpretation. And the I Ching is a parlor game.

As a parlor game the I Ching is lots of fun. Because of the psychological and moral depth of the oracles, an I Ching session can be a significant, illuminating exercise in social interaction and self-revelation.

However, as a solitary, diurnal ritual, the I Ching can be a neurotic and ineffectual shortcut to decision for individuals whose anxious indecision leads only to inaction: our *mal de siècle*. Used in this way, the I Ching is a compulsive act, the meanings of the hexagrams are obscure and unfelt, and the ritual becomes a substitute for normal reactions to experience.

π is the symbol for Tao, the Way. It is a gateway. It is the gateway through which we are constantly passing. We are never before the gate, nor beyond it. Nothing exists except there, with us, at the moment, in the gateway. We are always on the path, we are always in the Way, we are always in Tao—even if we don't feel that we are. Any conceptualizing by Taoists beyond this (and this included, of course)—the formulation of the Yin and Yang principle itself, for example, is karma, dogma, in a sense—means that it is a particular pattern chosen from the infinite number of patterns in the universe.

Anything that has meaning is restricted in this way. Meaning is an ordering of forms chosen from an absurd and formless void. Systems of meaning chosen from a point of view close to the meaningless truth will involve an enlightened and all-embracing religious concept and reflect the totality of existence more than systems devised from other meaningful systems and other forms and concepts. The Yin and Yang principle, for example, reflects the constantly changing, dying, and rejuvenating universe more perfectly than does Darwin's theory of the survival instinct. And Darwin's survival instinct and the theories of conservation of energy more perfectly reflect an undivided and entire universe than do theories of political or economic policy. By discovering the meanings of the deeper, closer systems, we discover more of the totality of experience. This is the secret behind all magic systems. They attempt to encompass in themselves all possibilities, so that the vision of existence seen *within* the system will be as perfect a reflection as possible of the All *without*. The greater arcana of the tarot, the zodiac, the palmist's chart, the I Ching, etc., are each a microcosm of the range of human experience.

None of the Eastern ways of enlightenment is strongly deterministic. But even the Zen Buddhists are sometimes reduced to using the concept of "reaction," implying *some* connection between moments. (This seemingly inevitable incapacity to sustain enlightenment into the process of verbal communication is due to the conceptual, historical base of language.) The Taoists speak of one's way through the omnipresent gate as having a direction. To accept this direction and move naturally in it is the pious desire of the Taoist. (Ideally, of course, he is without desire.) Hesitation, anxiety, dissatisfaction are to the Taoist what sin is to the Christian. To dispel them and clear the mind and heart the I Ching is devoutly, ceremoniously cast. The resultant hexagram indicates to the questioner his Tao, his natural direction, in the case of the particular problem that is stymieing him.

Strictly speaking—metaphysically—there are, of course, an infinite number of Taos. (Or, if you wish, only one Tao.) But in order to reduce the concept to a realizable ritual experience it was necessary to divide the range of Ways into a knowable, finite number of prototypes. After a short history of trial and error, sixty-four was found to be the most convenient number. (The mathematics of the system requires a square number.) Under what can only be regarded as divine inspiration the sixty-four hexagrams were formed into sixty-four examples of different ways of life, ways of being that covered the entire range of human experience. The sixty-four hexagrams essentially represent the same totality represented by the twelve astrological signs, the twenty-two cards of the major arcana and, to the palmist, the naturally formed geometry of the human hand. These hexagrams are not determined by the counting off of sticks or the falling of coins, but are determined by the forces of Yin and Yang within the individual. These are represented in the I Ching by broken (— —) Yin and solid (———) Yang lines composed in a vertical pattern of six.

Yin and Yang only roughly correspond to the Western duality of feminine and masculine, to which they are most often compared. An examination of a few of the ways in which the Yin and Yang differ from our polar concept of feminine and masculine reveal the skeleton of another polar concept: East and West.

The Yin/Yang principle represents the constant change and motion of the universe and thus of human experience. I Ching can be translated as "The Book of Changes." Ideally, as you cast the I Ching, you meditate on a problem, a question, a concept, or even a nonverbal feeling, which you have considered at length previously. It is a question which is part of you and the answer you seek is also part of you. The question and its answer are just two adjacent steps in your Tao. As you meditate on this particular problematic aspect of your experience, as you place yourself on the path of your question, you cast the I Ching. The lines of the hexagram will fall naturally in the Tao of the casting ritual. If the casting ritual is in the Tao of the question it is also in the Tao of the answer. Ideally, the meaning of the hexagram will have the feeling that it has been on the tip of your tongue the whole time.

The rituals of casting off yarrow sticks or throwing coins are not magic, but only mechanical means whereby the pattern of the forces that shape the Tao can be determined. The coins can be thrown in less than sixty seconds. It takes between half an hour and an hour to cast off the yarrow sticks. There is much more opportunity for meditation when the sticks are cast. As the lines

_E A S T_		_W E S T_	
Yin	_Yang_	_Feminine_	_Masculine_
feminine	masculine	feminine	masculine
negative	positive	negative	positive
yielding	strong	yielding	strong
follower	leader	follower	leader

But

dark	light	light	dark
secular	divine	divine	secular
action	inspiration	inspiration	action
rational	impulsive	impulsive	rational
square	circle	circle	square
heavy	buoyant	buoyant	heavy
body	soul	soul	body

slowly fall into place the questioner takes them into account; he moves painstakingly, deliberately, and relentlessly in the path of the question/answer. As the questioner carefully counts off by fours his right-hand heaps he already knows what the result of the counting off will be: this is a kind of check against the suspense or excitement of the divination breaking the flow of his meditation. He casts the sticks in solitude and in a spirit of religious acceptance. He may pause from time to time if he catches his mind wandering or if he is distracted. He knows that only if the sticks are cast in the spirit of the question will they indicate a hexagram that has meaning in terms of the question. If the coins are cast in the same spirit they too can indicate meaningful hexagrams.

Although the sixty-four hexagrams encompass all of human experience, the verbal formulations of this experience in current interpretations, translations from the Chinese, rely on Chinese cultural evaluations of the experience. The I Ching is a hodgepodge of Chinese culture from pre-Taoist wisdom to Confucianism and even more decadent, Machiavellian-type philosophies.

The traditional final version in present use was directed at Mandarin lords and their courts, whose problems, experiences, values, and symbols were radically different from ours. This gives the modern user of the I Ching a sense of obscurity and exoticism which is directly counter to the matter-of-fact religious philosophy behind the divination and the direct, down-to-earth character of the book. "He should be a guest at court." "Assert the right by force of arms." What do these admonitions have to do with the peaceful pothead in the woods of Vermont, the love-struck Bennington sophomore, or the small businessman in the grip of a political vise? Nothing. They are advice to the Mandarin courtier. They make a discrimination in the range of human experience which, although sensible in terms of its intended audience, is only vague and disquieting in terms of a modern audience. In interpreting the I Ching anew I have not changed the meanings of the hexagrams, but have changed the language of the interpretations so that they speak to you and me, in terms we can understand, in consideration of the realities (so to speak) of our present situation in history.

Method of the Yarrow-Stick Oracle

A bundle of fifty sticks is used. Yarrow stalks cut to the same length are traditional for the oracle. Except for the equalizing of lengths nothing else is done to them and each retains its individual shape, size, color, and texture.

1. Hold the bundle in the left hand.
2. Remove one stick with the right hand and set it aside.
3. Divide the bundle into two random batches.
4. Set one batch on your left and one on your right.
5. Take one stick from the right-hand batch and place it between the pinkie and ring finger of your left hand.
6. Grasp the left-hand batch between the thumb and forefinger of your left hand.
7. Reduce this batch by counting off bundles of four sticks with the right hand. Set these aside in a single discard pile.
8. When four sticks or less remain, place them between the ring finger and the middle finger of the left hand.
9. Grasp the right-hand batch between the thumb and forefinger of the left hand.
10. Reduce this batch as in step 7.
11. When four sticks or less remain, place them between the middle finger and forefinger of the left hand.
12. The total number of sticks in the left hand is now either nine or five. Set them aside in a separate remainder pile.
13. Using the sticks in the discard pile as your original bundle repeat steps 3 to 11.

14. The total number of sticks in the left hand is now either eight or four. Set aside in a second remainder pile.
15. Using the sticks now in the discard pile as your original bundle repeat steps 3 to 11.
16. The total number of sticks in the left hand is again either eight or four. Set them aside in a third remainder pile.

The first line, the lowest line of the hexagram, is now determined by the number of sticks in each of the three remainder piles.

A remainder pile with a total of nine or eight sticks has a value of 2; a remainder pile with a total of five or four sticks has a value of 3.

Add together the values of the three remainder piles. The resulting line is indicated as follows:

$$\text{Three 2s} = 6 = \text{---x---} \text{ (a moving Yin line)}$$
$$\text{Two 2s and one 3} = 7 = \text{--------} \text{ (a Yang line)}$$
$$\text{One 2 and two 3s} = 8 = \text{---} \ \text{---} \text{ (a Yin line)}$$
$$\text{Three 3s} = 9 = \text{---o---} \text{ (a moving Yang line)}$$

To determine each of the remaining lines of the hexagram, going from the lowest to the uppermost, repeat the entire ritual, steps 1 to 16, using the entire bundle (including the stick first cast off in Step 1). When the entire process has been repeated six times, once for each line of the hexagram, the hexagram stands revealed.

Method of the Coin Oracle

Use three coins. Toss them together. Each toss indicates a line of the hexagram, from bottom to top. If traditional ancient Chinese coins are used they will have an inscribed side and a blank side. The inscribed side has a value of 2; the blank side has a value of 3. If Western coins are used, heads is 3, tails is 2. Total the values of the three coins. The lines are determined as in the equations above (from "Three 2s" to "Three 3s"). The coins are thrown six times for the whole hexagram.

Moving Lines

The principle behind the I Ching is change: the inevitable change of a Yin force into a Yang force and vice versa. These changes are represented by the moving lines:

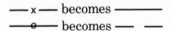

the 6 line ——x—— Old Yin
the 9 line ——o—— Old Yang

Most casts will reveal at least one moving line.

Moving lines indicate how the present Tao, represented by the hexagram cast, will change to another, represented by a second hexagram.

Moving lines change to their opposites:

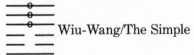

——x—— becomes ————
——o—— becomes —— ——

The second hexagram is formed by the stationary lines of the first hexagram and new lines resulting from the change in the moving lines. For example, hexagram 25:

Wiu-Wang/The Simple

changes to hexagram 24:

Fiu/Returning

When divining the hexagram the questioner reads the oracles for the moving lines as well as the general oracle for the hexagram. In the above case, in the hexagram Wiu Wang, he would take into account the oracles for 4 (——ө——), 5 (——ө——), and 6 (——ө——). (Lines are numbered from bottom to top.) As long as you understand that only the moving line cast by you applies to you, there is no stricture against reading the oracles and interpretations of the other lines of the hexagram. This will often clarify the meaning of the applicable line.

If a hexagram has no moving lines then the situation is either static or at an abrupt end and only the oracle for that particular hexagram is consulted.

Form of the
Interpretations

For purposes of simplicity and relevance the interpretation of each hexagram is divided into three sections, making liberal and inexact use of the names of three Hindu principles: artha, kama and moksha.

The artha section deals with more than the pursuit of prosperity, which is what is implied by the Hindu term. It deals with the questioner's relationship to other people, to authorities, and to "things" in his practical life. Any problems about courses of action within society are covered by this section.

The kama section deals with more than the pursuit of sexual pleasure, which is what is implied by the Hindu term. It deals with love relationships, either sexual, familial or involving close friends. For no other reason than to avoid conscious or unconscious confusion caused by the genders of pronouns, a character, Friend, is postulated to represent the other person involved in the relationship with the questioner.

The moksha section deals with striving for liberation—the exact meaning of the Hindu term. It indicates the proper spiritual path for the questioner at this juncture and also may reveal blocks and inconsistencies in his present philosophical position.

Trigrams

The earliest means of obtaining the oracles of what later was to become the I Ching was the reading of a tortoise shell. The method used by the ancient magicians is in dispute. In one version the tortoise shell was baked until it cracked and the pattern of the cracks was read to determine the oracle. In another version the configurations naturally appearing on the shell (each as distinctive as a fingerprint) were read.

The evolution of the I Ching began with a simple Yang or Yin, Yes or No, oracle:

——— Yes   — — No

With the addition of another line above the first, the yes/no oracle was modified:

═══ Yes   ═ ═ No

═ ═ Yes, but . . .   ═ ═ No, but . . .

With the addition of a third line there occurred eight possible oracles, eight figures of three lines each: the trigrams. Each of these eight trigrams was given a name and certain attributes were ascribed to it, relating to the position in the trigram of the Yin and Yang lines.

═══ Heaven   ═ ═ Earth

═ ═ Thunder   ═ ═ The Deep/Water

═ ═ Mountain   ═══ Wind/Wood

═══ Fire/Sun   ═══ The Marsh/Mist

The hexagram is a pair of trigrams and the course ascribed to each hexagram derives from the qualities of its trigrams and their related positions. For example, hexagram 14, ☲☰ (over), is the trigram Fire/Sun ☲ over the trigram Heaven ☰. The sun is the greatest treasure of Heaven. The force of fire is upward and it rises naturally into heaven, which already contains the sun. And Heaven is the symbol of the spiritual as opposed to the material. Thus hexagram 14 is the hexagram of wealth without greed, possession without desire.

The ancient interpreters also took into account a second pair of trigrams, the intertwining "inner trigrams" formed by lines 2, 3, and 4 and lines 3, 4, and 5 of the hexagrams.[1]

A table of the eight trigrams, a few of their attributes and their symbolic place in certain meaningful categories follows.

Use this chart for finding the number of the hexagram you have cast. Connect the upper and lower trigrams.

---

[1] See the works of Richard Wilhelm for more on the inner trigrams.

Trigrams:	Heaven	Earth	Thunder	Water/The Deep
Attributes:	Inspiration	Faithfulness	Impulsiveness	Danger
	Power	Submissiveness	Provocativeness	Labor
	Aggressiveness	Charity	Experimentation	Flexibility
	Completeness	Protectiveness	Vehemence	Melancholy
	Coldness	Evenness	Influence	Pervasiveness
Familial:	Father	Mother	Eldest Son	Middle Son
Animal:	Horse	Cow	Dragon	Pig
Anatomical:	Head	Solar Plexus	Foot	Ear
Element:	Metal	Soil	Grass	Wood
Color:	Purple	Black	Orange	Red
Season:	Early Winter	Early Autumn	Spring	Winter
Direction:	Northwest	Southwest	East	North

Trigrams:	Mountain	Wind/Wood	Fire/Sun	The Marsh/Mist
Attributes:	Inertia	Subtlety	Enlightenment	Happiness
	Perfection	Fragmentation	Clarity	Pleasure
	Inevitability	Formality	Warmth	Magic
	Modesty	Purity	Community	Destruction
	Carefulness	Transitoriness	Communication	Sensuality
Familial:	Youngest Son	Eldest Daughter	Middle Daughter	Youngest Daughter
Animal:	Dog	Cat	Bird	Sheep
Anatomical:	Hand	Thighs	Eye	Mouth
Element:	Stone	Air	Fire	Flesh
Color:	Green	White	Yellow	Blue
Season:	Early Spring	Early Summer	Summer	Autumn
Direction:	Northeast	Southeast	South	West

U P P E R

Trigrams:	☰	☷	☳	☵	☶	☴	☲	☱
L	1	11	34	5	26	9	14	43
O	12	2	16	8	23	20	35	45
W	25	24	51	3	27	42	21	17
E	6	7	40	29	4	59	64	47
R	33	15	62	39	52	53	56	31
	44	46	32	48	18	57	50	28
	13	36	55	63	22	37	30	49
	10	19	54	60	41	61	38	58

Reference Hexagram Chart

I Ching

1

Kh-Yen ▪ Yang

	Heaven below	*Heaven above*

O R A C L E

Heaven in motion;
the strength of the dragon.
The man nerves himself
for ceaseless activity.

Creative activity.
Influence.
Improvement.
Keep to your course.

I N T E R P R E T A T I O N

A r t h a ▪ The trigram *Ch'ien* is Heaven. Since there is only one heaven, the two trigrams represent heaven in change, heaven creating itself. This perpetual regeneration without attrition or waste is symbolized by the dragon. You ride the dragon of time with the primal, positive Yang force—enlightening, inspiring, strong, and spiritual. You are the center of activity. The positive, impelling elements of your life emanate directly from you, yourself. You give the direction and meaning to the Yang force of a circle of people and events around you. You make your own world just as the heaven below (heaven past) creates itself (heaven future) above. You are in constant motion and in harmony with the universe. You are not able to hesitate, you cannot change your direction, you cannot reduce your force. You reflect the constancy, inflexibility, and totality of the Yang force itself. If this hexagram, without modification by moving lines, really represents your Tao, then your consultation of the I Ching could only have been for purposes of affirmation—not because of indecision, hesitation, or lack of clarity on your part.

K a m a ▪ The Yin/Yang symbol takes its form from the practice of kama: it is a symbol of sexual union. In the practice of Artha, in one's day-to-day activities, the importance and power of the Yin force is always overshadowed in favor of the Yang force because of the illusions of progress, time, evolution, improvement, etc. But in love the roles of the inspiring and inspired are equal. The impetus of your relationship with Friend, the inspiration for its cohesive, passionate love derives from you. It is unlikely that Friend is as totally involved in yielding to your inspiration as you are in creating that inspiration. Because of your overpowering, totally impelling role in the relationship, Friend may feel put off, coerced, or frustrated in certain circumstances. Friend may have active impulses that conflict with yours. Although this is unavoidable, it need not be disastrous. Accept such conflicts; then give them little thought. This is the best reaction to your persistent disharmony.

M o k s h a ▪ Your role in spiritual matters is the enlightenment of others. You see no "ors" or "buts" in your spiritual vision. You cannot imagine an alternative to your own spiritual path. For you, there are no paradoxes. Enlighten others; let them see the unity in their discordant spiritual ideas. Enlighten others, so that the alternate paths they ponder will resolve themselves into a question of semantics. Enlighten others, so that paradoxes will become symbols for them, instead of problems.

L I N E S

1. —o— The dragon lies hidden in the deep.
   Take no action.

Your Yang power is still submerged and not yet ready to move out into the world of people and events. Its influence is still indirect. You cannot yet affect the action of others by your will. You will know the time is ripe for you to act when you find yourself taking action naturally, spontaneously, instinctively. Do not force anything. Do not will anything (except reserve and patience) at this point.

2. —⊖— The dragon appears in the field.
    Confer with the great man.

Your Yang influence is beginning to manifest itself in the world of people and events. You should seek out someone at the center of your sphere of activity, someone who has great influence. You will naturally combine forces with him.

3. —⊖— By day he is active and vigilant.
    By night he is careful and apprehensive.
    Danger
    but no mistakes.

Although your Yang force is unlimited, its direction is determined by certain social or cultural values that you hold. This is the reason that you experience anxiety, even though essentially you are so strong. If you cannot slough off illusions of right and wrong, if you still hold to the concept of future time, if you still imagine alternatives to reality, then you will not be able to fully feel the unlimited power you have or fully realize it. There is danger here of feelings of failure, unhappiness, and discontent, and also a danger of causing harm to others. Although such dangers are due to the coupling of your totally creative life with an unenlightened state of mind, they are not due to any conscious meanness on your part.

4. —⊖— The dragon leaps up from the deep.
    No mistakes.

You feel drawn in two directions. One is the way of public service, where the influential element of your Yang force takes precedence. The other is the way of holiness, sainthood, total withdrawal from the material world, where the light-giving elements of your Yang direction take precedence. Choose your path without being influenced by other people's values and needs. Remain true to yourself. Then whatever you choose will be right.

5. ──o── The dragon wings through the sky.
    Confer with the great man.

You clearly are an important person. Your influence is eagerly acknowledged by all. Your advice is universally sought. You have attained the point where you, yourself, personify for others the impelling creative Yang force that moves us all.

6. ──o── The dragon overreaches.
    Guilt.

There are limits to your influence. There are boundaries to the area of activity that you control. Do not attempt to carry your influence into spheres where circumstances and events have not led you naturally.

All moving ══o══ A swarm of headless dragons.
lines   ══o══ *Auspicious.*

Six moving lines indicate a perfect balance in you. Mind and body, objectivity and subjectivity, masculinity and femininity, activity and passivity, etc., all are in balance.

2

Kh-Wan · Yin

Earth
below

Earth
above

O R A C L E

The earth contains and sustains;
the qualities of a mare.
The man should not take the initiative;
he should follow the initiative of another.
He should seek friends in the southwest;
he should disavow friends in the northeast.

Creative activity.
Influence.
Improvement.
Keep to your course.

I N T E R P R E T A T I O N

A r t h a · Your course is totally Yin. It is entirely directed by an inspiring creative force outside you. It is important
to see your relationship with this active force not as a passive one,
but as a responsive, receptive one. *K'un* in no way implies
inaction—on the contrary. The earth is dependent on the sun for
its power, but it is not the sun that bears and nourishes, grows
and decays, expands and contracts, freezes and flows. Do not
confuse Yin with the Western concept of "feminine," which is
inactive, as opposed to masculine/active. Yang represents the
powers that direct and impel action. Yin represents action directly. You are responsible for activity in time and space, inspired

by an inactive, impelling force beyond dimension. The radiant dragon in heaven is the symbol for hexagram 1, *Kh-yen*. The mare—earthbound, in motion, docile—is the corresponding symbol of this hexagram. In moments of meditation, at times of inspiration when you open yourself to receive the impulses of the creative force that inspires you, you must be in solitude, alone with your yielding mind, without interference from others. In times of action in the material world you must join with others and attune with them to carry out the creative impulses that inspire you.

K a m a ▪ Recognize that Friend is the creative, inspiring force behind your relationship. You must respond fully and sympathetically. It is your responsibility to fulfill the relationship on a material, physical, sensual plane. Inspired by Friend's beauty, Friend's spirit or Friend's mind, you blossom and wilt, caress and withdraw, take hold and let go in an entirely selfless and sympathetic response to Friend.

M o k s h a ▪ You respond naturally and in complete sympathy with a creative spiritual force outside of you. Because of your completely yielding nature you approach Buddha's stricture to be without desire. Lose yourself in the spiritual revelations you have experienced; and follow, without compromise or equivocation, the impulses of these revelations.

L I N E S

1. —x— The dew has frozen.
   Winter approaches.

You perceive that your situation is becoming static. Steel yourself to the fact that this trend is irreversible. Face up to the fact that you are approaching a dead end. It is unavoidable.

2. —x— Straight, square and great.
   Success comes easily.

You maintain a perfect equilibrium between your Yin and Yang forces. Such an equilibrium negates all inner force, both imaginative (Yang) and pragmatic (Yin). Your life is not static, however, but flows in sympathy with the forces that surround you.

3. — x — The man is modest, but firm in his excellence.
        Like the king's mare,
        he does not take the initiative,
        but is the agent of the king's success.

You must actively repress the expression of those qualities in yourself which are most admired by others. These qualities should be revealed in your actions alone, not in your conversation or social relationships. Be secretively modest. In this way you can avoid the interference of adulation that would otherwise hamper your effectiveness.

4. — x — The sack is tied up.
        No guilt.
        No praise.

Refrain from expression of any kind. Move through the world as if in a dark, sewed-up sack. This is a time for complete detachment.

5. — x — Yellow lower garment.
        Very auspicious.

Yellow is the color of the earth. A yellow lower garment is a sign of reserve. When colors have meaning, clothes are carefully chosen. You must consciously, deliberately control your appearance with an eye to presenting an impression of modesty and reserve.

6. — x — Dragons battle in the wilderness.
        Their blood is purple and yellow.

You are resisting a natural change in your direction. An impulse to create, to inspire, has arisen in you. You regard it only as troublesome in your comfortable yielding, accepting position. By quashing it you not only weaken the potential of this new force within you, but you also undermine the ease and comfort you wish to preserve.

All Lines 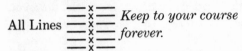 *Keep to your course forever.*

You move with the rhythm of the universal flux. Your emotions can be extreme, but they remain on this side of unhappiness— ranging from exuberant joy to blasé ennui.

3

Khun · Growing Pains

*Thunder
below*

*The Deep
above*

O R A C L E

The deep yawns above the thunder.
The man systematizes his life
with the care of a weaver at his loom.

Success.
Keep to your course.
Carefully consider any advances.
Seek assistance.

I N T E R P R E T A T I O N

A r t h a ▪ The Chinese symbol of this hexagram, *Khun*,
represents a plant struggling out of the earth. The trigrams
symbolize the beginning of the world, the tumultuous meeting of
the heavenly power of thunder and the earthly power of the
depths. The two dangerous trigrams, the danger of heaven
(thunder) and the danger of earth (the deep) have met with such
force that they have exchanged positions. You are in the midst of
the pell-mell confusion of the beginning of something, not of your
own doing, which has caught you up in it and has become the
major element in your life. If you see the situation as confused,
chaotic, difficult, and dangerous, then you are resisting your own
Tao. If you see it as full of potential, challenging and exciting,

then you are moving naturally in your Tao. Two admonitions: (1) Don't get involved in anything else outside of this situation: you must remain totally involved. (2) You cannot guide and influence a situation this involved and this far-reaching without the help of those whose goals and principles are sympathetic to yours.

K a m a ▪ The relationship between you and Friend is a new one. You've each brought to it many complications, both practical and emotional. Your chance meeting brought strong, new elements of conflict into both your lives; each of you feels he has been plunged into chaos. The sprouting plant straining against the crust of the earth and the tumult of a thunderstorm are both apt images for what is occurring. Don't panic—take things as they come, spontaneously and naturally. Don't overreact—keep a calm core throughout. Right now you are a lonely couple, although the uproar in your lives involves others beside yourselves. Together you must find mutual friends who will help you weather the storm.

M o k s h a ▪ You have just been plunged onto a new spiritual path. This is not a rational, natural outgrowth of your previous path. Some chance occurrence brought you into contact with this new metaphor of enlightenment and it was meaningful enough to you to draw you away from your previous spiritual course. Because this new revelation does not follow naturally from your previous metaphysical, religious beliefs, you may feel as though you have been uprooted—you may feel lost, confused, unsure. But there is no question that the strength with which this new spiritual system has gripped you is an indication of that path's correctness for you. Your spontaneous, welcoming reaction to it indicates that it strikes very deep chords in you, that it is a suitable way. You must search out others who are on this path; don't try to work it out alone. Consider yourself a blossoming neophyte and find yourself some mentors and guides.

L I N E S

1. —o— Advance is difficult.
      Keep to your course.
      Render assistance.

You have encountered an obstacle. It is correct to hesitate and take stock of the situation, but do not lose sight of your ultimate goal. While you are in this temporary standstill you should direct your energies toward the benefit of others.

2. —x— The horses rear, sensing ambush.
      Distressed, she tries to turn back.
      But the waylayer is not a marauder;
      he is a suitor for her hand in marriage.
      The woman keeps to her course and refuses him.
      In ten years she will marry and have children.

You find yourself under great pressures from all sides. Someone new has entered the scene. Under the burden of so many problems your first reaction is pessimistic; you think he comes antagonistically. Actually, he wishes to help you. He is sincerely, unselfishly interested in your welfare. His offer is tempting. But accepting his help would involve you in new complications and difficulties. You must refuse it. When you have your own life better under control—and that will take a long, long time—then you will be in a position to benefit from an involvement with someone else.

3. —x— Whoever hunts deer without a guide
      will lose his way in the depths of the forest.
      The superior man is aware of the hidden dangers
      and gives up the chase.
      If you advance
      you will regret it.

You have gotten yourself into difficulties by plunging alone into a new and strange situation. If you have the presence of mind to know that you lack the experience needed to deal with the forces that oppose you, you know that you must retreat completely or else become mired in failure and disgrace.

4. — x — The horses of her chariot turn back.
     She seeks assistance from her suitor.
     Auspicious
     if you advance.
     Improvement.

Potential aid is nearby. You cannot solve your problems alone, so you must swallow your pride and seek that aid. As long as you have chosen the right source for this aid, all will go well.

5. — o — The man should be generous,
     but difficulties confront him.
     Auspicious
     in small things
     if you keep to your course.
     Ominous
     in great things
     if you keep to your course.

Your intentions are good, but they are misunderstood by those whom you wish to assist. Although you have faith in what you are doing, do not undertake any contemplated action until you have gained the trust of others involved. You must proceed cautiously in what you do. Be patient, conscious of difficulties and sympathetic to the anxieties and fears of those you are trying to influence and aid.

6. — x — The horses of her chariot turn back.
     She weeps streams of blood.

The difficulties you encounter are too much for you. You have resigned yourself to defeat. You have become lost in chaos and disorder, not recognizing them as signs of the commencement of a new way, a new course for you.

4

Mang · Youthful Ignorance

*The Deep
below*

*The Mountain
above*

O R A C L E

From the deep at the foot of the mountain
a spring issues.
The man is resolute and takes care of himself.
I do not seek the ignorant.
The ignorant seek me.
I will instruct them.
I ask nothing but sincerity.
If they come out of habit
they become troublesome.

*Success
if you are firm.*

I N T E R P R E T A T I O N

A r t h a ▪ The attitude of the oracle to you is good-
humored, patronizing. Your innocence excuses everything. You
make faux pas that would humiliate most people; you make mistakes that would ruin others. But because of your youthful innocence your ignorance only amuses and refreshes those against
whom you blunder. This is the hexagram of "beginner's luck": the
neophyte who wins in card games, makes a killing in the market,
wins the heart of the reticent lady, creates primitive beauty that

speaks universally, etc. You are this kind of inexperienced, innocent person in your present situation. Ignorant of accepted
stratagems and theories, you are less limited in your action.
Unfamiliar with the conventions of the situation, you plunge
right in and deal with people as individuals. As long as you retain
this innocence everything you do will be either successful or
excused—even in your repetitive demands on the I Ching.

K a m a ▪ This is the hexagram of the innocent goatherd
Daphnis. Whether Friend, like Chloë, is as innocent as you or as
heartily sophisticated as Daphnis's guide in the practice of love,
Lycainion, your relationship will be happy and constantly re-
newed with sweet pleasure.

M o k s h a ▪ Your spiritual innocence, your lack of metaphysics and religious metaphor, endear you to those from whom
you seek enlightenment. They may find you frustrating as well.
You have the same kind of holy innocence exhibited by the cook in
Po Chang's Zen monastery. In order to determine his own successor, Po Chang asked his pupils to express the essential nature
of a particular pitcher. The monks gave various verbal and indirect answers. The cook approached the pitcher and kicked it to
the floor, breaking it, and he was named Po Chang's successor.
With the proper teacher you *can* reach enlightenment in your
present state of freshness and innocence. It is more likely that
you will eventually become involved in one of the systems of
images, ideas, and practices that make up the longer and more
conventional paths to spiritual freedom.

L I N E S

1. — x — The ignorant man must be dealt with severely
         and encouraged to open his mind
         if his ignorance is to be dispelled.
         Some guilt
         if you are too firm for too long.

You must discipline yourself if you wish to become adept. But this discipline must arise from your own need, at your own volition. Do not place yourself under the inflexible strictures of an existing system of discipline. Retain the freedom of innocence in choosing the means of your own self-discipline.

2. —o— The man puts up with the ignorant
         and has a way with women
         but he can fill his father's shoes
         when the time comes.
         Auspicious.

With your inexperience and ignorance you are still open-minded enough to deal warmly and patiently with fools—fools who cannot claim your excuse of youthful innocence and who are generally scorned and avoided by others. Your innocence gives you a way with the opposite sex and protects you from any unpleasant complications. Although inexperienced, you have the steady character and native intelligence to be able to take on grave responsibilities when the right time comes. This is the line of Prince Hal.

3. —x— The girl embraces the marble faun
         mistaking it for the real one.
         No success.

For success, love, or enlightenment you eagerly honor and emulate someone else who seems to exemplify what you seek. But in your youthful innocence you confuse your ideal of that person with the person himself. It is transparent that all your eagerness, ardor, and interest have little to do with the intimate human nature of the person you idolize, have little to do with how he sees himself as an individual. You will put him off permanently, and do yourself no good.

4. —x— Enchained in ignorance.
         Guilt.

Although innocent, you are full of anxieties—anxieties about your lack of experience. Natural, phenomenal beginner's luck cannot develop from such an attitude. Your anxieties will gain complete control.

5. — x — The barefoot boy.
      Auspicious.

You are trusting, optimistic, and patient. Good luck.

6. — o — The man whips the barefoot boy.
      Ominous
      if you take advantage of the ignorant.
      Auspicious
      if you protect the ignorant.

You have made a foolish mistake. If you become flustered and try to rectify it, you will make other foolish, thoughtless mistakes and become embroiled in an embarrassing comedy of errors. You cannot undo what has been done. Do not bother about it any longer, except to regard it as an example of what not to do, as a warning to prevent further mistakes.

5

Zhuy · Waiting

 Heaven
below

 The Deep
above

O R A C L E

There are clouds in the sky.
The man eats, drinks, and is merry.

Great success.
Auspicious
if you keep to your course.
You may cross the great water.

I N T E R P R E T A T I O N

A r t h a ▪ Waiting—not hoping, not expecting, not
fearing—just waiting. Whatever you are facing—an insoluble
problem, an overwhelming threat, or an impending conflict—is
entirely out of your hands. Although the problem is yours, its
outcome is completely dependent on the actions of others. Although the threat is aimed directly at you, only the threatener
has any control over its being carried out. If you are constantly
hoping for a way out, then you are living an unrealistic fantasy. If
you are constantly expectant, guarded, watchful, then the problem has taken over your life; instead of avoiding it, you have let it
consume you. If you are anxious and fearful then the problem has
already done its worst. Neither hope, expect, nor fear. And do
not act. Any action would be only a frantic, unreasonable expres-

sion of your hope, expectation, or fear, because it is impossible for you to affect the situation in any way. But if you wait, content with yourself and your life . . . if you wait in the present moment, fulfilling yourself completely in it . . . if you wait in the knowledge of universal perfection . . . then nothing and no one can have any effect on you in any way and you will be always free.

K a m a ▪ You and Friend are besieged by outside pressures. Your love for each other sprung up between yourselves; now, under attack from outside, it seems fragile and almost unimportant. You have conflicts now that you could never have imagined. Because your separate reactions to these outer pressures are different, you clash with and oppose each other. It is unfortunate that what is ideally a private matter has attracted the attention of others, but there is nothing you can do about it. If you love Friend, then love Friend day by day, hour by hour, minute by minute. Keep outside pressures and problems outside. When difficulties appear because of the nervousness, envy, or prejudice of others, meet them spontaneously together. If you and Friend remain tight, although you may suffer a buffeting, you will not break. If you allow circumstances to set you against each other, any major obstacle could be disastrous. This is the hexagram of Romeo and Juliet. Their marriage is a spontaneous reaction, based on love, of lovers to circumstance. Juliet's fantastic prevarication with the deadly drug is a confused and indirect act. It has no connection with Romeo. It is frantic reaction to anxiety about the future—the fear of marriage to Paris. With the love between you, you and Friend can well afford to wait things out.

M o k s h a ▪ You dwell on death. A vision of death as an ending, a loss, a definite, inevitable, and unforestallable destruction shapes your spiritual life. Such an image of death is maya, an illusionary concept based on the illusion of the ego. Death is not destruction. It is the continuation of changes in the constantly changing physical world. Your individuality? It is only a factor of man's complicated social processes. What you consider to be yourself—almost by definition "that which dies"—is a series of momentary forms in a flux without origin and without end.

L I N E S

1. —o— Waiting at the distant border.
   No mistakes
   if you are patient.

All goes well for you. Deep down you sense vague and distant portents of impending difficulties. Worrying about them will only bring them on more swiftly. Your worrying could give them power over you that they otherwise would not possess. Remain true to your present well-being. Do not let these indistinct images of an improbable future affect you.

2. —o— Waiting on the sand beside the mountain stream.
   Auspicious.
   Evil rumors.

Impending difficulties have caused conflict and dissension. You and your companions, anxious about the future, have begun spitefully to blame each other. You feel that the others wrong you. You feel that they act from their own feelings of guilt. Their hysterical search for a scapegoat angers you. Thus you reveal that you feel equally guilty and are equally hysterical. No one is guilty. Your impending problems come from outside sources— forces that will overwhelm you unless everyone comes together to defeat them.

3. —o— Waiting in the river mud;
   the man is vulnerable.

You act precipitously. You act from anxiety. You react to threats that are still only abstract. Wait. Wait and react spontaneously to whatever the present moment brings. By acting prematurely you force the threat to manifest itself; you bring about exactly what you wish to avoid. Caution and a sense of the seriousness of the situation may protect you.

4. — x — Waiting in a bloodied cave;
the man will escape.

Terrible and oppressive events are in store. The way to endure
them: Regard them as your fulfillment. Discover your Buddhahood.

5. — o — Waiting at the banquet.
Auspicious
if you keep to your course.

There has been a lapse in the outside pressures that assail you. It
is only a brief respite. The situation is far from its conclusion. But
give yourself a break. Forget the problem for a while. Do not get
involved any further until you must. Relax. Concentrate on the
pleasures of your life and your positive activities. When outside
pressures begin to burgeon you will be able to react with re-
newed wisdom and strength gathered during your moment of
peace.

6. — x — Waiting no longer.
Three rescuers arrive at the cave.
Auspicious
if you treat your rescuers well.

You suffer the utmost despair in what seems to be an impossible
situation. To add to your problems, another, completely unforeseen element has arisen—something strange and unfitting, con-
fusing and disquieting. You do not know what to make of it. You
feel so defeated that you are prone to treat this new thing negatively, cynically. But if you meet it respectfully, seriously, and
without prejudice, it will reveal itself as a way to your own
liberation.

6

Sung · Conflict

*The Deep
below*

*Heaven
above*

ORACLE

Water tends to move earthward,
away from heaven above.
In a situation where there is strife
the man knows how important first steps are.
Even though he is sincere
he will meet with opposition.

*Auspicious
if you are cautiously apprehensive.
Ominous
if you let strife come to a head.
Confer with the great man.
Do not cross the great water.*

INTERPRETATION

A r t h a ▪ Although your values may seem like absolutes
to someone with a strong character, from a philosophical point of
view all values are relative. You feel deeply that what you believe
and what you do are right. And, in your terms, you are right—
but, in *their* terms those with whom you disagree are also right.
From an objective point of view, your values, your aims, and
your actions are only a few among many elements and processes

of the overall pattern of human reaction and interaction. As a balance to your positive, steadfast attitude you must retain this objective "other vision," whose truth you instinctively feel. Remember that your adversaries are also in the grip of personal absolutes—immovable and inflexible. Without lowering your standards or hedging on your principles, make an effort to meet them halfway. Since both sides are implacable, you must find a wise mediator with the authority, either civil or religious, magical, philosophical, or social, to decide the question once and for all. This particular conflict was formed the moment you entered into the relationship(s) involved, which indicates that you must be more judicious when initiating situations. Until the conflict is resolved, do not undertake any of your more ambitious enterprises or make any major changes in your life.

K a m a ▪ Why do you insist that Friend be like you and speak and act and breathe according to your vision of the world? It's egotistical—and obviously absurd. Your complementary personalities are what brought you together in the first place; now, instead of being the reasons for your loving they have become the reasons for hating. You must let Friend be true to Friend's self. As Friend will be, anyway—just as you are true to yourself . . . but in strife and deceit? or in love and calm reaction? Each of you has a distorted view of himself. Go to a third party with a disinterested viewpoint—not just a mutual friend, but a professional counselor, an astrologer, a psychiatrist, a yogi. Or refer together to a book or to music or to a film for which you share a common sympathy. Do not dally with other relationships until you and Friend have begun to reconcile your differences.

M o k s h a ▪ You are not spiritually free because you cling anxiously to one metaphysical image of the Universe. You feel threatened by other concepts of God. But every system is a reflection of the One and All. All beliefs and all denials of all men are only sequined mirrors on His robes.

L I N E S

1. — × — The man shies away from conflict.
   Auspicious
   after the rumors die down.

Since the conflict is still in the budding stage, the best thing for you to do would be immediately to break completely with those involved in the troublesome relationship. You will suffer some verbal abuse, but all will end for the best.

2. — o — The man is not equal to the contest.
   He retires, disguised, to a small town.
   No guilt.

You are up against great odds; perhaps you should back down— all the way. Trust the values you place on responsible action and your own survival. Withdraw. The humility you feel will touch all the elements of your life so that in the end you will feel no bitterness. Treating everyone, even enemies, with humility and compassion you will find you have withdrawn not in rage, but in peace.

3. — × — The man holds his ground.
   He draws his reputation around him like a cloak,
   and makes no major effort.
   Those who depend on him
   do not appreciate his sacrifice.
   Auspicious
   but perilous.

Most of your possessions—spiritual or material—are yours simply because you acquired them and continue to hold them. If they are lost, stolen, traded, or destroyed, they no longer belong to you. There are a very few, however, which, because they were created by your own mind or hands or because of your persevering devotion to their attainment or through love, more than just belong to you; they have become a part of you and will remain so. Your expansive personality exposes these most meaningful possessions and they are always threatened. It may seem that one of them has been taken from you—an image has been plagiarized, an idea usurped, a lucky fetish lost. But although it is in the possession of others, it is still yours, irrevocably and eternally. So remain content with that. Do not make a fool of yourself by trying to recover it or seeking retribution. Your right to it cannot be proved and it will seem to others that you are exaggerating its value, making a mountain out of a molehill. If you are in the service of another, do not undertake any new responsibilities.

4. ——o—— The man is not equal to the contest.
He withdraws from the contentious world
into the peace of spiritual devotion.
Auspicious
if you keep to your course.

You see a conflict with someone else looming ahead of you. You know that if you engage in the dispute you will eventually be victorious, but you still cannot bring yourself to disrupt your life in that way. Even though your cause is just and you are capable of carrying it out, you have withdrawn in favor of peace and quiet. If you remain steadfast in your decision, without regrets or recriminations, all will be for the best.

5. ——o—— The man in the very midst of battle.
Very auspicious.

The words and opinions of someone in your circle carry great weight. This person would be an acceptable arbitrator of your difficulties with others. If you have no moral or ethical reservations about your own aims, his judgment will be in accord with them.

6. ——o—— If the king honors the man with a leather belt,
before the morning is over
it will have been taken from him three times.

You may feel that you have finally triumphed in some way. But no, it is not final. This victory of yours will only lead to another reaction and you will soon find yourself in the midst of the same conflict again . . . and again . . .

7

Shuh · Soldiers

The Deep
below

The Earth
above

O R A C L E

The earth covers the deep.
The superior man nourishes and educates the people,
making soldiers of the multitude.

Auspicious
with no mistakes
if you keep to your course
guided by experience and age.

I N T E R P R E T A T I O N

A r t h a ▪ This is the hexagram of Mao Tse-tung. He fulfills the oracle directly by bringing true the letter of its symbolism. In a more personal sense, the hexagram indicates that you must find support and assistance among the many people who surround you. They are no help to you whatever right now. You must apprise them of the oppressive situation, inculcate them with your point of view, convince them of the need to take action, and provide them with the strength—material and moral—to act. If you are someone whose age and experience automatically demand respect, then you will find it easier to be accepted as a leader.

K a m a ▪ You and Friend are well matched but as inmates of a rarefied cultural atmosphere, with absurd ideals and ambiguous values, you are both under a constant debilitating strain. You and Friend must "get away from it all," rediscover yourselves as people; you must cut the ties that bind you and begin to live quietly, simply, and patiently. Then you will discover the essential human bonds of your love.

M o k s h a ▪ As you move on the path to enlightenment your life changes with your successive revelations; your revelations change your motivating principles and change your vision of the world. In order to live in accordance with your present religious principles, you must now become one of the people. It is not your mission to make your revelations known to others, but to broaden your own spiritual life by experiencing the basic spiritual revelations common to all human beings.

L I N E S

1. — x — The soldiers set forth under orders.
      Ominous
      if the orders are not good.

You have prematurely set in motion the forces you have amassed. You have neglected to double-check your strategy. And you have neglected to measure the honesty and humanity of the principles behind your actions.

2. — o — The leader is among the soldiers.
      The chief commends him three times.
      Auspicious.
      No mistakes.

You receive public awards and honors. To accept them is neither hypocritical nor unfair. You are a symbol of the success of those who honor you. Your honor is inwardly shared by everyone.

3. — x — The soldiers in the wagons are dead.
      Ominous.

Miscalculating your strengths, denying your weaknesses, you have set forth on a path of inevitable disaster.

4. — x — The soldiers retreat.
No mistakes.

Ultimately you will overcome. Now you must withdraw and wait for a time more suited to action.

5. — x — There are birds in the field.
It would be wise to seize and destroy them.
The eldest son is sent to lead the soldiers;
his officers are idle young men.
Ominous
if you keep to your course.

You have been given the responsibility of leadership. You have done well as a follower, but you do not have the strong qualities required in a position of authority. You have let your personal life intrude on your public life. Instead of providing yourself with experienced advisers and skillful administrators, you have surrounded yourself with friends who fill their positions as poorly as you fill yours.

6. — x — The great ruler appoints his governors of states
and chiefs of clans.
Small men should not be used.

You have overcome the oppressors. But have you yourself become the perpetrator of the same old oppressions? or the perpetrator of new injustices?

8

Pee Seeking Union

*The Earth
below*

*The Deep
above*

ORACLE

The deep covers the earth.
The ancient kings divided the land into states
and fostered friendship among their princes.

*Auspicious.
Cast the oracle again to determine
whether your mind is great, unremitting, and firm.
If it is, no mistakes.*

INTERPRETATION

A r t h a ▪ You are the creation of a culture, of a society, of a brotherhood of shared experience, and of a family. Even your own individuality is only a concept that—like all others—owes its existence to the community of man. You cannot "find yourself" by avoiding close association with your brothers. Join in something people are doing, if the principles behind it fit your own. It is neurotic to believe you might "lose something of yourself" if you become a member of a group. Let yourself go—the experience of being in close sympathy with others, pursuing common goals or common pleasures, will give you a better perspective on yourself and your problems.

You may feel anxious about the welfare of your fragile sensibilities if you should become a true, integral member of a group. These fears will diminish as you approach taking the step that will unite you with others. If you hold off indefinitely the time will come when you will literally be incapable of closeness to others. Your shell will have become impenetrable—from within as well as without—and you will be irreparably cut off from your brothers. It could be that you have the qualities to become the cohesive central force of such a group. A demonic personality and a sense of purpose are required. If you feel that perhaps it is in your Tao to devote yourself to gathering others around you in a spirit of sympathy and community, cast the I Ching again. Then decide whether or not you're really up to it.

K a m a ▪ There is a third entity to every pair—the mysterious third character on arcanum 6 of the tarot (the Lovers): there is you and Friend and "we," i.e., both of you together as one. This third entity—we as lovers—gives strength and structure to your relationship. You each have an equal responsibility to it. If you are so involved with other affiliations that you have decided to let Friend take care of the business of loving, then you weaken the relationship.

M o k s h a ▪ As long as you do not recognize every man as your brother—you will not find it. As long as you do not recognize that every table is your brother—you will not find it. As long as you do not recognize that the midnight sky is your brother—you will not find it.

L I N E S

1. — x — Sincerely seeking union.
   No mistakes.
   Improvement
   if you are filled with sincerity.

Form your relationships only on the basis of sincere sympathy with others. Strength and solidarity will result. Beware of inconsiderate motivations.

2. — × — Instinctively seeking union.
          Auspicious
          if you keep to your course.

Respond naturally and freely to the desires of others. Do not fawn on them, trying to anticipate their desires.

3. — × — Seeking union with unworthy men.

Through habitual socializing you have become an intimate member of a group not really sympathetic to your own principles and values. You must withdraw from this group. There is no harm, however, in remaining on congenial terms with individual members of the group.

4. — × — Seeking union with a greater man.
          Auspicious
          if you keep to your course.

You are in close, sympathetic contact with someone at the focal point of a community, someone to whom others look for strength and guidance. Do not be embarrassed to express your feelings to him. But beware of being swayed from your own principles.

5. — o — The highest example of seeking union:
          the king urges the hunt only on three sides;
          the game escapes before him.
          His people join in his example.
          Auspicious.

Do not coerce anyone to become part of your group. Do not condemn those who do not wish to. This will assure that all attachments are free and sincere.

6. — × — He seeks union
          but has not even taken the first step.
          Ominous.

You are guilty of the dangerous prolonged hesitation cautioned against in the "Artha" section above.

9

Zhiao-Khuh · Minor Restraint

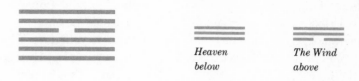

Heaven
below

The Wind
above

O R A C L E

The winds of heaven:
the great air currents carry the weather.
They come from the west
bringing dense clouds, but no rain.
The superior man adorns himself
as an outward manifestation of his virtue.

Success.

I N T E R P R E T A T I O N

A r t h a ▪ You are far behind the advance of changing times and fashions, changing generations and changing events. You are carried along, willy-nilly, powerless to resist or to make any changes yourself. Any active moves you make cause only conflict, not change. Any efforts you make to disentangle yourself only entrap you more. Any attempts you make to deal with the forces that direct the course of your life only result in your being left even farther behind. Only in your outward bearing, in your manner, in your appearance, in your behavior, can you freely express yourself without fear of conflicts or embarrassment.

K a m a ▪ Because of your love for Friend you acquiesce to demands made by Friend that go against the grain, that rankle, that disturb and embarrass you. These demands are so important to Friend that any resistance to them would be met by extreme anxiety and hostility on Friend's part. If your love is strong enough for you to act against your own principles, then continue to give in freely, without resistance, and with affection and good grace. If you cannot set to rest your inner opposition to Friend's impulses, then you should not have anything at all to do with Friend.

M o k s h a ▪ Powerful and far-reaching illusions have control over your Tao. They inhibit your spiritual life at every turn. If you are an artist, you are caught up in clichés. If you follow a guru, you are caught up in hero worship. If you *are* a guru you are caught up in pride. If you are a Christian, you are caught up in self-righteousness. If you are a Buddhist, you are caught up in passivity. If you are a magician, you are caught up in fantasy. If you are a Freudian, you are caught up in your ego. You must give up your spiritual ambitions. By following the other, "lower" paths of existence according to unselfish, humanitarian principles, you will eventually reach the point where you can break through the conceptual dead ends that now entrap you on the spiritual plane.

L I N E S

1. ——o—— The man turns back
   to his proper course.
   There can be no harm in that.
   Auspicious.

You cannot accomplish what you are attempting. Forget it. Return to the way of life you had before you undertook your ill-fated project.

2. ——o—— The man is drawn back.
   He keeps to his proper course.

Auspicious.

Those whose aims and directions have so far coincided with yours have regressed, have withdrawn, leaving you alone. You cannot see any reason for their pulling back. But unless you feel that you are definitely at the point of achieving your objective, you had better follow the example of your colleagues and withdraw as well, immediately.

3. ──◦── The strap that holds back the carriage has been
        removed.
        The man and his wife avert their eyes.

Taking advantage of the mildness of others you are attempting to influence a situation forcefully. Because of your overbearing and cynical attitude, your efforts have met with indignant resistance. Even those who, until now, have been sympathetic and encouraging find fault with your aggressiveness. You bicker with your friends. There is little you can do.

4. ──x── The man is sincere.
        Bloodshed is avoided
        and his anxieties are quelled.
        No mistakes.

Contrary to the first sentence of the "Artha" section above, you are *not* far behind the vanguard of changing events. You are close to the people and institutions that direct the changing trends of values and ideas. If you wish to counter the prevalent drift, take action; it will be effective. You may be called upon to use extreme measures; no matter what they are, they are not as extreme as what would occur if you were to remain inactive.

5. ──◦── The man is sincere;
        he attracts loyal allies.
        The man is resourceful;
        he has the wealth of his neighbors.

You have good friends. Between such friends there is mutual sympathy and a mutual need for each other. Recognize this as a blessing and cultivate your friendships openly and with no inhibitions.

6. ——⊖—— Rain has fallen;
   progress is delayed.
   The man appreciates
   the progress he has made until now.
   The woman is in a state of peril,
   no matter what she does.
   She is like the nearly full moon.
   Ominous
   if you take any action.

In your inoffensive, meek reaction to objectionable forces you have withdrawn to the point where those forces have hardly any influence on you at all. You must be very careful to remain passive and impassive to authority, and not to attempt to break completely free. Although the temptation has presented itself, to attempt a break for complete individual freedom would be to break the Tao, the method of mildness that has brought you to the point of being nearly free. The moon, however brilliant, is always a Yin force—receptive, reflective. Although it is able from time to time to free itself from the encroaching darkness, because of its Yin nature it cannot sustain its unfettered brightness. As soon as the moon is full it immediately begins to wane. Do not rush yourself headlong back into subjugation.

10

Lih · Treading

The Marsh
below

Heaven
above

O R A C L E

The sky above, the marsh below.
The man discriminates between high and low
and acts in accord with the wishes of the people.

You tread the tail of the tiger.
It does not bite you.
Success.

I N T E R P R E T A T I O N

A r t h a ▪ You try to be discriminating in your personal
acquaintances—in fact, you're something of a snob. Perhaps because you react deeply to other personalities, or perhaps because
you are not fortified enough to take the pressures of social contact, you shy away from most personal confrontations. You have a
few close friends who share your values, your serious attitude
toward life, and very often your tendency toward aloofness.
More mundane social contacts try your patience and disturb your
tranquillity. The circumstances of your life force you into these
disturbing contacts every day. There is nothing immoral or un-
democratic in discriminating as you do, as long as you understand
that your judgments are based on your own personal needs,
inclination, and taste. Beware: over a period of time you may

come to regard your evaluation of others as judgments of universal principles. You may begin to feel *superior* instead of just *shy*. You will not hurt others by this attitude—to them you will only appear fatuous and impolite. But you can hurt yourself. Regarding your subjective evaluations as universal principles will harden you toward others and close you off to spontaneous social experiences. You will lose touch with the small surprises of love and friendship that can occur naturally in your daily routine. Danger: prejudice.

K a m a ▪ You have reconciled yourself to the fact that you and Friend have different opinions of each other's activities. Friend does not take seriously what you do and vice versa. You have reconciled yourself to this, so it in no way diminishes your love for Friend. However, there is a danger that you could begin to feel superior to Friend, to judge Friend as well as Friend's inclinations, and to think of Friend as frivolous or evasive. This kind of wrongheadedness can diminish love; it conceptualizes the relationship and imposes abstract ideals on a real person. Under these circumstances you no longer *see* Friend, you *observe* Friend; you no longer *touch* Friend, you *examine* Friend; you no longer *know* Friend, you *possess* Friend. Friend can be compared to a porcelain figurine which, although judged by its owner to be tasteless and mawkish, still holds for him a sentimental meaning that perpetuates his warm attachment. As the porcelain figurine is loved for its past associations and not for its essential form, you love Friend for similarly self-centered reasons, without giving credit to Friend for any innate attractiveness. Beware! Do not forget that the differences between yourself and Friend are complementary. Each of you brings equal value to the relationship.

M o k s h a ▪ You feel you have achieved a level of understanding beyond the reach of most people. Even those on the same path as yourself seem to be very far behind you. You have reached out to them, but they seem to remain embroiled in matters of dogma and paradox. Do not judge them. The fact that you *desire* to elevate them is proof that you are far enough away from the enlightenment you suppose you approach for there to be little qualitative difference between you. You are right here with everyone else—on the wheel of karma.

1. —o— He treads the familiar path.
    No mistakes
    if you advance.

You have the opportunity to distinguish yourself by accepting a public responsibility. Is your desire for this honor an expression of your inner self? Or is it born of fantasies of exaltation, privilege, and power? Beware.

2. —o— A quiet, solitary man
    treads a level, easy path.
    Auspicious
    if you keep to your course.

You are not involved in the rat race. You are free of the anxieties and doubts that attend others in pursuit of their insatiable desires. You are content and never become involved in personal conflicts.

3. —x— He has one eye and thinks he can see well;
    he is lame and thinks he can walk well;
    the braggart acts the part of a great ruler.
    He treads on the tail of the tiger
    and is bitten.
    Ominous.

Considering his physical deficiencies it would be foolish for a one-eyed man or a lame man to perform such a dangerous stunt as treading on the tiger's tail. You either ignore or are blind to the fact that you bring to your situation debilitating personal liabilities which doom your efforts. Not only will you fail, but you will provoke an unfortunate reaction.

4. ——o—— He treads on the tail of the tiger
with the utmost caution.
Auspicious
in the end.

You have taken on a seemingly impossible task. Outwardly you
seem to be going at it in fits and starts, cautiously, hesitantly;
inwardly you have the strength and direction of purpose to carry
it through. This is the line of Abraham Lincoln.

5. ——o—— He treads resolutely.
Peril
if you keep to your course.

You are resolute and persistent in your chosen direction. You are
also aware that it can lead you into conflicts with others. Try to
skirt these conflicts or to mitigate them. Prepare for them.

6. ——o—— *Examine the course you are treading*
and see where you are going.
Very auspicious
if your goal has now been reached.

You have completed something and now wish to know if the
ultimate consequences will be what you anticipated. Look back
and examine the incidental results that accompanied your past
efforts. If you approve of these past results, then the ultimate
consequences of your actions will also meet with your approval; if
you do not approve of your methods, then it is unlikely that the
end results will meet your approval either. The Tao of the work is
in the Tao of the working.

11

T-Hai · Peace

Heaven
below

The Earth
above

O R A C L E

Heaven descends.
Earth ascends.
They join.
Heaven and earth mingle within the man.
The wise man brings this accord to the people.

Auspicious.
Success.

I N T E R P R E T A T I O N

A r t h a ▪ As you cast your sticks or coins for this oracle
you experienced peace of mind. While reading this you may be
full of the anxieties and expectations that arise from your question, that are your problem; but while casting the hexagram, in
the act of performing the ritual, you were at ease. In order to
establish a correspondence between the patterns in an individual
life and the patterns of the coins or sticks the questioner should
concentrate on his question while casting the oracle. You, however, became so involved in the "doing" of the oracle that while
casting it (before you reached for the book) you entirely forgot
your problem. The ability to get totally involved in what one is
doing at the time one is doing it is a rare gift. Cultivate this kind

of total involvement. Extend it to all your activities. It is a path not so much of calm as of order, where your life's concerns do not overlap, where you can concentrate completely on the most immediate activity.

K a m a ▪ You are not totally involved with Friend. You do not share your entire life with Friend. You include Friend only when the situation seems to relate to Friend on an obvious level. Everyone has certain close and secret places; but you keep too much of your life hidden from Friend. Perhaps you have a tendency to keep the unpleasant, problematic things to yourself and share only the pleasant things. If Friend is not like you the different situations and problems and events in Friend's life which probably overlap yours require a response. Thus, although the meaning of this hexagram is peace it could bring about conflict.

M o k s h a ▪ Your spiritual path is the regular practice of certain rituals. These rituals will not lead directly to your enlightenment. But because of your total involvement in them, rituals symbolizing a union with the One and All will indeed unite you with the One and All as you perform them. Without enlightenment, without the usual dramatics and self-consciousness that accompany loss of ego, while performing your rituals you are in Nirvana—egoless, formless, mindless.

L I N E S

1. ——o—— He pulls up a cluster of wildflowers;
   the grass comes with it.
   Auspicious
   if you advance.

Your ability effectively to concentrate on what you are doing attracts others who have the same goals, if not the same gift of total involvement. This can only further your efforts. Accept these friends.

2. —o— He can put up with boring men.
   If there is no boat he can swim the river.
   He has almost total recall.
   His friendships are based on love.
   He certainly keeps to the golden mean!

All things are equal. Act with consistent principles. Treat
strangers like friends. Undertake difficult things as naturally
and spontaneously as you undertake ordinary, workaday things.
Do not make a distinction between things close to you and things
distant—anything that involves you must be met with the same
principles of objectivity and fairness, without evaluation or prejudice.

3. —o— No union without disruption;
   no departure without return.
   No mistakes
   if you keep to your course,
   foreseeing difficulties.
   Do not let inevitable changes distress you;
   savor the joy of the present.

The oracle is clear. To "savor the joy of the present" is to know the
relativity of all joy and sorrow. Remain calm while dealing with a
situation which, for the moment, overpowers you.

4. —x— He joins with his neighbors
   and does not rely on his wealth.
   His neighbors join with him
   without fearing his power.

Because you are free from persistent anxieties, you have a sincere, unprejudiced approach to whomever you meet. You are
open and sincere with the most casual acquaintance. Those who
know you appreciate this.

5. —x— Prince Yi made a new rule
   when his daughters were married.
   Happiness.
   Very auspicious.

By the decree of Prince Yi, the daughters of emperors were to obey their husbands just like other wives, although they were usually of a higher rank in court. Whether in a love relationship, a business relationship, or any other relationship, you can make a similar kind of accommodation in your life. You can successfully reconcile conflicting principles by dividing your life into different spheres of activity, such as—in the case of Prince Yi—the world of the court and the world of the family.

6. — x — The wall joins the moat.
The man is not aggressive;
he plots with his allies.
Some guilt
even if you keep to your course.

While following the natural course of your life from immediate present to immediate present you have been careful to separate one activity from another. You thus ignore the possibility of interaction between them. A moat surrounding a wall should ensure double fortification. But a moat planned without consideration of contingent factors may be dug too close to the wall. If the wall topples it will fill the moat. Past thoughtlessness makes you vulnerable. Do not attempt to defend yourself. Withdraw to your inner circle. Accept your fate.

12

P-Hih ▪ Disjunction

The Earth
below

Heaven
above

O R A C L E

Heaven and earth separate from each other.
There is a lack of understanding between men.
The great ones have gone
and the small ones have come.
The superior man conceals his true qualities
and avoids calamities.
He shuns gainful employment.

Difficulty
in keeping to your course.

I N T E R P R E T A T I O N

A r t h a ▪ You live in a world informed by petty principles:
greed and possessiveness, selfishness and resentment, competi-
tion and hatred, etc. Money is the treasured excrement (using the
image of N. O. Brown), the useless waste, of this situation. Stay
away from it. In your particular situation the vulgar, materialistic corruption is so far-reaching that you can be drawn into it
inadvertently by the acceptance of money from anyone. In this
hexagram the trigrams of Heaven and Earth draw away from
each other. If you are not a saint or monk practicing moksha,
hitched to receding heaven, you are here on earth, a madman
among others delighting in their own effluvium. Your situation is

without the traditional restraints of charity or humane social ideals for the future. Those with whom you are involved could be vicious. If you *have* any unselfish principles, restrain yourself from advancing them—they can do no good. They will be completely misunderstood and bring not the faintest ray of light to others. Content yourself with holding those principles intact within yourself—you will find that alone difficult enough to do.

K a m a • Only in the loose terms of a confused language could your relationship with Friend be called a "love" relationship. You conflict in pettiness; you unite in pettiness; your pains are petty; so are your pleasures. Small and mean, if not demanding, resentful of each other, you have completely lost track of the basis of your relationship.

M o k s h a • This is the hexagram of St. Simeon Stylites, the pillar saint who lived for thirty-five years on a small platform atop a pillar in the Syrian desert. In a culture where the very language is often confused and righteous acts are always misunderstood, only such an absurd life as St. Simeon's is recognized as being spiritually inspired. Materialism is so desperately all-consuming in your world that only a life of asceticism bordering on the absurd can free you for your spiritual path.

L I N E S

1. — × — He pulls up a cluster of wildflowers;
            the grass comes with it.
            Auspicious.
            Improvement,
            if you keep to your course.

You are being carried away by events that at first glance seem not to concern you directly. Do not resist or try to extricate yourself. Purely by accident you are being swept out of the reach of a danger you have not yet even recognized.

2. — × — Patience and submission.

> *Auspicious*
> *for the small.*
> *Success*
> *amid suffering and obstruction*
> *if you can make this your course.*

You are closely involved with the greedy and mistrustful culture. You have been lucky so far just to have been able to hold your own, being constantly on the defensive. The destructive, inhumane situation expressed by this hexagram could be a blessing, if its unredeemed meanness were to impel you inward. There you can find the success of a content, accepting life.

3. — x — He is ashamed of his intentions.

The fact that everyone else is involved in the same shameful situation makes it more bearable for everyone. Unfortunately, this justification cannot mitigate your guilt. Its only effect is to prolong the situation.

4. — o — He acts with piety
and makes no mistakes.
His friends come
and share his happiness.

Although success is unlikely, if you wish to act on your principles, go ahead. To act boldly and sincerely will not cause you too much trouble at this point and by doing so you may encourage others to do so as well.

5. — o — He brings suffering and obstruction to an end.
A great and fortunate man.
"Watch out, watch out!" he cries,
tying his success
to the stump of a mulberry tree.

Within the stiffest, most static, and most shapeless life there lies the potential for growth and creativity. But first—self-awareness.

6. — o — Suffering and obstruction are conquered.
From now on, happiness will increase.

Anything, no matter what, is better for you than the situation expressed by this hexagram. So be glad. You have come through.

13

T-Hung-Zhan · Society

The Sun below

Heaven above

ORACLE

A fire beneath the open sky.
The superior man distinguishes things
according to their kinds and classes.

Success,
if you keep to your course.
You may cross the great water.

INTERPRETATION

A r t h a ▪ The principles that underlie the social contract
are the principles that direct your own life. You agree explicitly
with Aristotle's definition of man as "a political animal." Although you recognize the existence of certain inequities within
every society, you regard them as necessary to its structure.
Whatever you do is done in this context: confidence in and sympathy with the social structure. Not confused by the prevalent
ambivalence of loyalties to one's individuality and to society, you
are able to fulfill your role in society and enjoy fully whatever
benefits accrue from the natural workings of the social mechanism. This hexagram in no way implies any oppression of you or
brainwashing or naïveté on your part. The society of men, their
joining together for mutual good, their building of social struc-

tures that have an architectural sense of balance, support, and finality are reflections of the gathering of the All into the One.

K a m a ▪ You and Friend see your relationship as an archetypal one. If you are lovers you see yourself as "the Man and the Woman"; if related, as "the Mother and the Daughter," "the brothers," etc.; or as "the Teacher and the Student"; or as companions, as Mind and Body, etc. Your relationship is not simply one between two individuals. You feel a natural bond to the *idea* of your type of relationship, with its set rules for each member and its traditional areas of conflict, as it has manifested itself in culture. You may be interested in the work of C. G. Jung. This way of being together makes strong and lasting bonds between yourself and Friend; you understand each other perfectly; although somewhat didactic, neither of you is selfish or dishonest. You each feel a sense of historical responsibility to fulfill your roles to each other in a way worthy of your archetypal counterparts.

M o k s h a ▪ The society of all things as it is reflected in the tumultuous society of men is the idea that illuminates your path to enlightenment. History inspires you; inspired, you begin to see history as myth; as myth it reflects divine patterns and enlightens you. Reading is your ritual, e.g., the *Bhagavad-Gita*, the most inspired presentation of this spiritual idea; Homer; *The Golden Bough*. The seemingly endless lists of names in the Old Testament have a beauty and meaning for you that they do not have for others. You remain aloof from the stresses and convulsions within your own social structure and see the human condition from above, seeing man as ultimately united in the patterns of the One and All, beyond good and evil.

L I N E S

1. ——o—— He unites with other men
   in his own doorway.
   No mistakes.

Your having joined with others is not the result of a sudden heartfelt appreciation of the joys of society. A situation common to you and the others has impelled you into this group. Although your presence in it is almost inadvertent, you should remain and work in it.

2. — x — He unites with members of his own family.
   You will regret it.

Your social sphere is too limited. In a situation that requires companionship with all, you have joined only with some. This is snobbish and narrow-minded and will be regarded as such by others.

3. —o— He hides his weapons in the grass
   and crouches at the top of the hill.
   He does not make a move for three years.

You have taken the first steps toward entering a certain community, group, or organization which is an unselfish society of men with a common cause. Yet you do not fully believe in the sincerity and integrity of the group. You are suspicious. Not having fully thrown off the bonds of the idea of the individual, you cannot believe that others have done so. You hold yourself aloof from the others. You have prepared yourself to strike back if someone tries to take advantage of you. It will be a long time before you can bring yourself fully to enter this community, and a long time before you are accepted in it.

4. —o— He mounts the wall to do battle,
   then sees no need to defend himself.
   Auspicious.

You are about to let yourself go and fully enter into an unselfish, rewarding society of men. You still retain some feelings of competitiveness and wariness, but it has begun to dawn on you that these feelings are truly absurd.

5. —o— He is forced to unite.
   At first he wails and complains;
   later he laughs at his own distress
   and meets with his conqueror.

You have joined in a strong union with others. This union is highly structured and causes you many hardships at first. You are not used to the new constraints and responsibilities that accompany membership. When you do become accustomed to them you will find your life easier than before, with fewer anxieties, fewer practical difficulties, and more ease and joy.

6. ——o—— He unites with men in the suburbs.
    No guilt.

The suburbs of a city are a kind of Limbo. This line expresses the fellowship of those in Limbo. Without a common goal, without a common past, with nothing in common but being equally lost and cut off from other men, you have joined with others in similar straits.

14

Teh-Yuh · Wealth

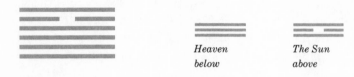

Heaven
below

The Sun
above

O R A C L E

Fire above heaven.
The wealthy man represses evil and honors good,
in the spirit of divine law.

Great success.

I N T E R P R E T A T I O N

A r t h a ▪ This is the hexagram of wealth without greed;
of possession without desire; of material fulfillment without an
appreciation of it. *Blessed are the meek: for they shall inherit the
earth.* Your mildness, your inoffensiveness, your lack of competitiveness, your circumspect ego, your simple realistic values, all
endear you to those who know you. Compared with you *they* are,
to one degree or another, aggressive, competitive, and greedy.
As a kind of tribute to your meekness, as a kind of payoff for your
not being a threat to anyone else's ambitions, material wealth
is allowed to accrue to you. But wealth isn't what you desire. You
do burn with a desire for something, although you don't generally acknowledge it to yourself. In your meekness you cannot
recognize the form of your own fulfillment. (See "Moksha" section.) And so you become encrusted with castoffs from the material fulfillment of others.

K a m a ▪ Friend is a perfect lover. Friend is beautiful, un-selfish, exciting, tender—it seems as if you should be deliriously happy. But you are not. You feel that something is missing; a certain sympathy, a certain closeness of contact, a certain depth of love in your relationship. But this lack is not due to Friend's neglect—it is due to yours. You are so meek, so afraid to show your feelings, that the relationship is a one-way one, with you on the receiving end. Friend's desire toward you *is* to be a perfect lover. You must discover what your desire toward Friend is, and express it.

M o k s h a ▪ *Blessed are the meek: for they shall inherit the earth.* But what about heaven? Your material success is an incidental consequence of your spiritual meekness. A *major* con-sequence is that there is no chance of your experiencing religious joy. Casting this oracle may well have been your first step in the spiritual realm. You generally ignore your moksha—the spiri-tual side of your life. You pretend it doesn't exist. But the answer to your problem, the solution to your unhappiness, lies there. It is the form of the unrecognized fulfillment mentioned in the "Artha" section. Is it a fear of failure in this most important matter that keeps you from delving into it? But there is nothing to fear in moksha: everyone, everything in moksha is kind. It is time to discover who you are.

L I N E S

1.   —o— *No mistakes*
       if you keep yourself from harm.
       No mistakes
       at the end
       if you see the dangers and difficulties.

Right now you are accruing possessions without impinging on your own principles. As you continue, though, you will sooner or later be called on to compromise yourself. Do not.

2. —o— The large wagon
    has a full load.
    No mistakes
    if you advance in any direction.

Do not become attached to real property or any other kind of
cumbersome possessions that could inhibit your activity. If you
remain free of such binding attachments, you can undertake
whatever you wish.

3. —o— A prince presents himself as an offering.
    A smaller man could not do this.

If you keep what you have, your wealth will be a burden to you. If
you give away what you have, your wealth will bring you joy.

4. —o— He conserves his resources.
    No mistakes.

If you attempt to match the opulence of others, pride or envy will
lead you to make mistake after mistake in your business and
social affairs. You must live without imposing comparisons on
your life.

5. —x— Mutual sincerity.
    Auspicious
    if you act nobly.

Because you are unselfish and humanitarian, with the means to
be generous as well, you act with a certain self-assured ease and
familiarity that ignores social conventions and offends some of
your friends and colleagues. If you wish to avoid these conflicts,
you must accept certain codes of behavior. Although of no value
to you, still they have value for others.

6. —o— Heaven helps him.
    Auspicious.
    Improvement
    in every way.

You recognize a saint. You give him help. You partake of his
wisdom. Good fortune.

15

Kh-Yen ▪ Modesty

 The Mountain
below

 The Earth
above

O R A C L E

The mountain recedes behind the horizon.
The modest man is successful by nature.

*Balance your impulses
for an objective judgment.*

I N T E R P R E T A T I O N

A r t h a ▪ First of all, you should be modest in your behavior. There are a few people whose immodesty is condoned and accepted by others; you are not one of them. But there are deeper kinds of modesty and immodesty and the latter may be responsible for the pitfalls you are encountering. Certain aspects of self-consciousness can be considered as immodest. Perhaps you are so full of your most important projects and activities that you relate *all* your experiences and *all* your personal contacts to them. Besides the misunderstanding and even resentment on the part of others this single-mindedness may cause, it also distracts from your efforts to accomplish your great project. It takes away from it the immediacy and the objectivity necessary to a productive approach. Or perhaps you spend your time imagining the details of the culmination of your efforts; daydreaming under the guise of "planning." This is also immodesty. It is immodest to place yourself on a level above your activity, to feel that you can look down from above at what you are doing. When you step back to observe what you are doing, when you talk about what you are doing, when you think about what you are doing, then you are observing, talking, thinking—but not doing. What you are doing is no longer an integral part of what you are; it is only an idea. It is the dark glass through which you see yourself. If there is some activity for which you are particularly suited, do not gloat or plot or fantasize about it. It is a gift from God. Get down to it.

K a m a ▪ You feel that you understand your relationship with Friend and attempt to direct it according to your understanding. Perhaps this is a conscious activity: consciously, verbosely perhaps, you work out the different levels and changes of the relationship, putting pressures on yourself and Friend to conform to your ideal. Perhaps it is unconscious. You may pride yourself that you are "trying to work things out" while what you are doing is imposing neurotic, sentimental expectations on the relationship. Love is an absolute, but like other absolutes it loses its absolute meaning as soon as it is spoken. Love is all-embracing, but as soon as it is named, it is limited. As soon as lovers speak love, they limit their love by implying the possibility of not loving. As soon as lovers think love, they begin to see themselves as "lovers," instead of as real people. The situation is seemingly inevitable to some extent. But such immodesty should not be encouraged to overwhelm the entire relationship with a lovers' ideology.

M o k s h a ▪ If you see yourself as enlightened, then you are considered by others to be enlightened; you are both wrong. If you do not see yourself as enlightened, then you are not considered by others to be enlightened; you are both wrong. And, in either case, you are aware of the anomaly.

L I N E S

1. — x — Modesty upon modesty.
    Auspicious.
    You may cross the great water.

If you are leading a quiet, purposeful life, in a manner both honest and inoffensive toward others, you can successfully and happily take any great step or make any major change in your life that you wish. If you feel a conflict with anyone, or an ambiguity about any element of your life, then you are not prepared to take that step.

2. — x — Modesty apparent.
    Auspicious
    if you keep to your course.

You are free of false or self-conscious modesty and do not attempt to repress manifestations of your true modesty. True modesty is your major character trait. It is evident to everyone. You are entrusted with responsibilities because of it.

3. — o — Modesty acknowledged.
    Auspicious.
    Continued success.

You have accomplished something, both in your own eyes and in the eyes of the world. Along with other qualities, the kind of modesty spoken of in the "Artha" section above played a role in your success. Now that your achievement has been recognized by others, you may be modifying your view of yourself, which has been modest up to now. There is a danger of immodesty appearing in your contacts with friends and colleagues; or a danger of your fruitful activity being subverted by immodest and grandiose ideas. Just a small step in your persistent activity brought you the success you now enjoy; do not forget that the next step you take will be just as small.

4. — x — Active modesty.
    Improvement.

Modesty should not be an excuse for hesitation, for restraint, or for not fulfilling your responsibilities. You feel that you are too insignificant, too ordinary a person to assume certain responsibilities that are inherent in your role. This is only a rationalization for copping out. You live within a social system, whether you like it or not, and you have responsibilities that derive from that system. Remember, there are others who depend on your fulfilling your role.

5. — x — Modesty bringing influence.
His neighbor supports him.
Be aggressive.
Improvement
whatever you do.

You are essentially a modest person; however, it is now necessary that you act immodestly. You may be called upon to rise to leadership in some way; you may have to speak frankly and unreservedly with a friend; it may be necessary to expose part of your life to public scrutiny as you follow your Tao. Whatever principles propel you toward this immodest act are more basic and more important to you than the principle of modesty.

6. — x — Modesty bringing modesty.
Improvement,
whatever you do,
even if it seems against your best interests.

Conflicts that have arisen between you and your close friends are the result of immodesty on your part and on theirs. To hold back from exposing your mutual faults is only superficially modest and is actually irresponsible. You must make a show of humility, concentrate on your own faults, become an example for others, pointing toward a return to the love, the community feeling, and the sense of purpose that are the touchstone of your association.

16

Yih · Enthusiasm

The Earth
below

Thunder
above

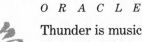

O R A C L E

Thunder is music to the earth.
The ancient kings composed music
in honor of their own virtue,
and presented it to God,
inviting their ancestors to be present.

*Rally your forces
and set them moving.*

I N T E R P R E T A T I O N

A r t h a ▪ This is the hexagram of music that moves. This is the music that gathers together and inspires feelings of brotherhood and common cause. It is music without pretension that seeks and woos and loves those who listen. It is not intellectual, classical music, but spontaneous music whose forms derive from a tradition of spontaneous music. It is music that unites those who play it and listen to it, elevating them. If you are a musician, this is the kind of music that you make. If you are not a musician, you still make this kind of music in whatever you do and inspire similar enthusiasm in those with whom you work or live or socialize. You are an instrument on which you, yourself, play—in an intense search for common bond and common mind and common breath among those around you. This is the hexagram of Adolf Hitler.

K a m a ▪ Your personality alone generates the vibrations of love and passion that inspire your relationship; Friend swoons dizzily along. This is the hexagram of Rudolph Valentino.

M o k s h a ▪ Music is the art of patterns in time; dance is the art of patterns in time and space. Music and dance can bring about ecstatic enlightenment as no other art forms can. There is a point when, in some forms of music, in some performances, the musician ceases to *create* patterns in time and begins to *reflect* the variety of the patterns of the universal flux. Listening to such music, becoming part of it, can bring union with the One and All. And dance enlightens through the reflection of the variety of patterns in space. In the music-dance ritual of ancient China, where ancestors were invited back to dance and sing, the music and dance, so in tune with the rhythms and shapes of the great flux, could weave itself through the barriers of Time and reach into the past. Joined with their reappeared ancestors in transcendent enjoyment of the same music the participants were united with the One and All. Consider these things, with the thought that music is your path to enlightenment. This is the hexagram of the Dalai Lama.

L I N E S

1. — x — He dances to his own tune.
   Ominous.

You act as if the world were hanging on your words and deeds, ready to follow you anywhere. Actually, it is either trying to escape your boorishness or is preparing to pounce on you.

2. — x — He is as firm as a rock.
   He has the gift of foresight.
   Auspicious
   if you keep to your course.

Although everyone else is being swept away by a new element in your situation, you yourself have not been carried along. You alone recognize that it is too early to perceive the real worth of this force; you hold back. This is the correct attitude. As soon as you sense something not exactly right, as soon as you catch a wrong note, you must immediately dissociate yourself from the source of the misled enthusiasm of the others.

3. — x — He sings for his supper.
You must understand!
Guilt
if your understanding comes too late.

Instead of giving yourself over to the fervent feelings that prevail, you are waiting for a sign from someone you consider to be your superior, a sign that he also feels this fervor. Meanwhile, you are being left behind.

4. — o — Harmony and satisfaction come from his music.
He enjoys great success in great things.
Great success.
If you do not doubt them, friends gather around.

You yourself are the source of the prevalent zeal. Everyone has been won over by your humility in the face of what seems to them the temptation to egotistically seize power.

5. — x — He is chronically ill.
He lives for a long time
on the verge of dying.

Because of certain problems and restraints you are unable to join in the prevalent fervor. But it is better to be in difficulties when everyone else is feeling good than to be in difficulties when many other people are in the same boat as yourself.

6. — x — He makes music mindlessly.
No mistakes
if you do not persist in your course
after its end.

You have been carried away by the success of your own charisma. You are caught up, with ego and without reason, in the fervor that originates from you yourself. This is a religious frenzy; it is an ecstatic dance to the music of the spheres. As long as you have enough presence of mind to "come down" when the trance, the communion, is over, the experience will be a valuable, maturing one.

17

Swee · Following

*The Thunder
below*

*The Marsh
above*

O R A C L E

Thunder rests in the marsh.
In the evening the superior man
goes home to rest.

*Great success.
No mistakes
if you keep to your course.*

I N T E R P R E T A T I O N

A r t h a · You are not a solitary person. The course of
your life depends on others for its accomplishment. You believe
that your failures are due to the faults of others, and you blame
your own faults on someone else's failure. This egocentricity
leads to enmity and misunderstanding. You believe that you do
your best most simply and happily to follow your course and that
you are constantly being hindered and distracted by the actions
of other people. But they too are doing their best; they too have
principles and aspirations—as do you—with differing degrees of
success and failure. Perhaps your goals and principles are too
unlike those of the people whose lives mesh with yours. This
could make you feel that your true direction, your right course, is
being obstructed by the contrariness of others. If you insist on

burdening yourself with set goals and static principles (see "Moksha" section), then you must at least adjust these goals and principles so that they will no longer conflict with the general goals and principles of your milieu. If you cannot accept frustration as inevitable then you must adjust your principles to more closely coincide with the values of those around you.

K a m a • When it comes to your relationship with Friend, the important and decisive principle in that relationship is the relationship itself, the love between you. In matters that involve Friend—and these *could be* everything that occurs in your life— the overwhelming consideration, the value basic to them all, is the honesty and openness, closeness and love between you. However, outside the relationship you and Friend have different sets of values and principles that often conflict with one another. But where Friend is involved there is only one overwhelming consideration and you must let the other, lesser things go. You must dispel expectations that disrupt Friend's own. You must not rankle spitefully; repressing your disappointment, when Friend, motivated by Friend's own goals and principles—just as valid as yours—spoils what were fantasy plans and dashes what were vain hopes. Place little value on any of your aspirations that interfere with the love between you and Friend; the frustration of such aspirations should be regarded by you as nothing more than small nuisances compared with the importance of attaining happiness with Friend.

M o k s h a • You understand the illusory nature of your goals and principles: you have liberated your mind. But you will not be enlightened until you liberate your activity, your behavior, your way of life as well. To achieve enlightenment you must completely throw off all ideologies no matter how broad, all principles no matter how humanitarian, all your values—even the highest. Once enlightened, the bodhisattva can return to the enactment of daily life based on principle because, free of his own principles and values, he can unreservedly and spontaneously be receptive to the goals and principles of society.

L I N E S

1. —⊸— The man turns from his pursuit
   and follows something else.
   If he goes beyond his own gate
   in search of followers,
   he will be honored.
   Auspicious
   if you keep to your course.

You have a harmonious relationship with those very close to you. Everyone else you exclude, prejudging them by the values of your clique. All your conflicts occur with those outside your intimate circle of friends. However, the attainment of your goals depends on your having cordial relations with those outside this circle. Instead of disparaging them, free yourself from your parochial viewpoint and open yourself up to these outsiders. Through understanding and appreciating those you now ignore or revile you can best achieve your aims, which are also the aims of the intimate, sympathetic coterie of friends that means so much to you.

2. —×— He follows the little boy
   and lets the man of age and experience go.

The principles on which you base your friendships should be the same as the principles by which you evaluate humanity. If not, danger.

3. —×— He follows the man of age and experience
   and lets the little boy go.
   He will find what he seeks.
   Keep to your course.

Within your own life you have conflicting principles and conflicting values. You must choose one direction and stick to it, letting the other go, aware that a passing sense of loss is unavoidable, and accepting it.

4. —⊸— He attracts followers.
   Ominous

if you keep to your course.
If you make your intentions clear,
how can you make a mistake?

Unintentionally you attract others to you. What you do and how you do it appeals to people. You are an object of emulation. Although your "Fame" is now only incidental to your life's course and the motives behind it, it will become troublesome unless you acknowledge it now. Although you are not concerned about the impression you make on others, still you are responsible to the following you have unwittingly gathered. Act freely, however you wish; just make your intentions crystal clear beforehand to your admirers.

5. ——o—— He encourages excellence.
           Auspicious.

The true nature of your course and the constancy of your principles assure you of a happy and beautiful life.

6. —x— He holds firmly to his cause;
           he clings to his cause;
           he is bound fast to it.
           The king presents his offerings on the western
           mountains.

Your life is determined by the expectations of those who follow you. It really becomes a question of who is following whom. The king in this oracle is a figurehead king bound to his role; he makes no personal choices, he has no personal motives; he acts entirely in the role of king as prescribed by tradition, the political advice of the court and the pressure of popular opinion. Modern parallels would be: the department head who cannot make decisions against the consensus of his department; a politician whose success depends on the support of his friends; a substitute seventh-grade teacher on his first day.

18

Kiu · Fixing

The Wind
below

The Mountain
above

ORACLE

Wind at the foot of the mountain.
The superior man helps others
and fortifies himself.

Success
if you keep to your course.
Cross the great water,
but for three days before doing so
consider the step carefully;
and for three days afterward
reconsider it.

INTERPRETATION

A r t h a · Disaster threatens you. At any given time any situation is part of a developing and changing larger situation that develops and changes under the influence of certain even larger, seemingly static situations: social mores, political practices, the climate, etc; and one's own personality is also a factor. When things go well you give credit to these larger factors. When trouble arises you blame them. The prime factor in your present situation, however, is neither fickle fashion, the establishment, or the weather—it is your own personality: confused, ambiguous, and dishonest. (1) Confused in your values, you misplace your priorities. Until now you treated your troubles lightly and gave them little thought; now they "suddenly" have become hopeless and overwhelming. (2) Ambiguous in your principles, you cannot take a stand. Your judgment is always tentative, equivocal, and your actions, therefore, are unclear. (3) You are most dishonest to those closest to you. You have no one to blame for your oncoming ruin but yourself. This is the reason why this is a very auspicious hexagram. Since, outside of your own weaknesses and failures, there are no other factors that have a strong influence on the situation, it is within your power to change completely your way of life. Without worrying about disruptive adverse outside forces, you can rectify the faults in yourself that have brought on your ruin. No halfway measures, no wheedling or manipulative compromises with yourself can help. (1) Recognize how serious your problem is and how extreme the ruin that approaches. (2) Plumb yourself to discover what your true and deep principles are. Apply them, no matter how inconvenient, unconventional, or embarrassing. (3) Apply the golden rule in your relations with others. This may mean a great change in your life, an upheaval. But this is the time to start, the time to "cross the great water." Danger: impatience. Do not be impatient with yourself if for a time you seem to lapse from your new resolutions. Do not be impatient with others if for a time they seem not to react to your new relations with them. The situation had been conditioned by what went before and will not change overnight. With patience and fortitude all will turn out very well in the end.

K a m a ▪ The "Artha" section applies clearly to your emotional life as well. Friend is capable of opening up to you, of helping you to change the guarded, hypocritical, anxious atmosphere of the present relationship into one of honest, understanding love. But you are the one basically to blame for your troubles; it is up to you to take the initiative. And again, do not be impatient.

M o k s h a ▪ You have not fully entered your chosen spiritual path. You have allowed selfish and egotistical drives to enter your spiritual practice. Not that you must be like Buddha, "without desire"—you are not ready for that yet. The paradox of a spiritual course is that the desire it is supposed to annihilate is implicit in the practice itself, which arises from a desire to eradicate desire. But there are other troublesome factors, less paradoxical and more mundane, that enter into your spiritual life; you hold ideals and desires contrary to your spiritual principles. You can make no spiritual progress until you abolish these irreverent and unprincipled considerations, this bad karma. Your feelings of conflict point directly to the elements of your life that should be eliminated. If something you do makes you feel guilty—stop doing it; if something you desire causes you anguish and anxiety—banish the desire; if when you speak you feel weak and vulnerable—remain silent. The practice of moksha must always be peaceful, without conflict. Your spiritual practice depends only on yourself.

L I N E S

1. — x — The man fixes
      what his father ruined.
      If he is successful
      the father escapes blame.
      Auspicious
      at the end
      after peril.

You rely too much on past principles; you are not reacting directly and honestly to the present situation. As time has passed you have changed gradually, passively, and imperceptibly. Now you must actively change. You must refresh and reform your principles. After you establish fresh principles of action you must act. First, reform the structure of your life. It is a necessity—a highly precarious one. Danger: carelessness. The changes you make will be far-reaching. The consequences of an unsuitable, thoughtless reformation can be disastrous.

2. — o — The man fixes
      what his mother ruined.

Do not go to extremes
in keeping to your course.

Some specific, very serious mistakes have led to your ruin. Besides changing your own outlook you must also undo these past mistakes. This will take time and patience. When dealing with other people you must understand their own troubles and not be too demanding. For a time yet people are liable to be suspicious of you—and understandably so.

3. —o— The man fixes
what his father ruined.
Some guilt
but no major mistakes.

The flurry of activity required to fix things may annoy others. In your haste you are bound to step on some toes. But the successful outcome of your frenetic activity will justify your thoughtlessness.

4. —x— The man overlooks
what his father ruined.
If you keep to your course
you will regret it.

Your situation has just begun to deteriorate; your troubles have just begun to form. You are not yet convinced of their gravity and are too indecisive to make the changes called for by this hexagram. Unfortunately, things will have to get much worse before you are literally forced to take some action.

5. —x— The man fixes
the ruin bequeathed by his father.
His efficiency in doing so
brings him praise.

Your mistaken attitude and the mistakes you have made that brought on your ruination are obvious to other people involved in them with you. They lay the blame for them on you and they are correct. Since they are so sensitive to you and what you do, they will react favorably, with relief and warm praise, if you make any effort to change the mistakes you have made.

6. —⊙— The man sees nothing to be fixed.
       He remains aloof
       and cultivates his own spirit.

You place little value on the situations and relationships that have
been ruined. Do not try to deal with them. Confine yourself to
situations and relationships which do not cause conflict between
yourself and others.

19

Lin · Conduct

The Marsh
below

The Earth
above

O R A C L E

The marsh within the earth.
Fertile soil.
The superior man is always nourished,
always nourishes others.

Success
if you keep to your course.
Ominous
for the eighth month.

I N T E R P R E T A T I O N

A r t h a ▪ Anything from accidental happenstance to your
own willful application has given you authority over other people.
It could be the kind of authority that comes from controlling the
funds of others or the kind that comes from a universal recognition of your wisdom and honesty. It could be authority bestowed
from above or below. Act always alert to your power. Use it
paternally, munificently. Whatever is the context of your authority is something new and fresh; it has only loose ties to tradition.
The enterprise you lead is in its spring. Like Dionysus, after
raising the full fruits of summer, you will "die" in the sense that
your power will die. Afterward, you will be resurrected. In the

Greek myth only Dionysus's heart was saved. His avatar after resurrection was his own living heart, ensconced and cherished in a pretentious temple. In the same way, you can expect a winter restitution—to a place of honor, this time—not to authority.

K a m a ▪ You dominate Friend; Friend submits to you. It is not neurotic, since both of you are aware of it and enjoy it. This arrangement carries you to great heights of passion and pleasure. But Friend will tire of this game before you. The resulting conflicts are obvious. Compromises of love will lead to eventual reconciliation. But it will never, never be the same.

M o k s h a ▪ You have been finding your own way. You have been experiencing revelations; your vision of the universe is changing. You are changing too. Every experience is like a doorway into a new room; in each new room you take your harmonious role. This is a burgeoning, a blossoming for you—a natural metamorphosis—intellectual, not biological. It is a transition from one form to another. It does not last long and after it is over all your subsequent development will take place within the confines of your new, static form.

L I N E S

1. ——o—— He shares the responsibility
          with the man who follows him.
          Auspicious
          if you keep to your course.

You are very much in step with the times. Whatever is on your mind is soon on everyone else's mind. Things come out well for you with very little conflict. Be careful. Do not lose yourself in the momentum.

2. ——o—— He shares the responsibility
          with the man he follows.
          Auspicious.

> *Advance.*
> *Improvement, whatever you do.*

You lead a harmonious and successful life in the material world while at the same time possessing an enlightened and devout belief in the transitory nature of all earthly things.

3. — x — He is eager to act
   but his action will be futile.
   Anxiety
   but no mistakes.

You have freed yourself from pressures and cares that others still experience. Your easygoing attitude offends them. Rectify it with a little friendly reserve.

4. — x — He acts well.
   No mistakes.

You are in an atmosphere of honest and sympathetic communication.

5. — x — He acts wisely
   like a great chief.
   Auspicious.

If you include others in your life, respectfully keep in mind that they are including you in their lives.

6. — x — He acts with honesty and generosity.
   Auspicious.
   No mistakes.

You have been in spiritual seclusion. You should now reenter the world and transmit to others the visions that have enlightened you.

20

Kwen ▪ Contemplation

The Earth below

The Wind above

O R A C L E

The wind blows above the earth.
The ancient kings matched their regulations
with the customs of the different regions.
The worshiper has washed his hands
but has not yet presented the sacrifice.

*Keep to your course
with a dignified bearing
that commands respect.*

I N T E R P R E T A T I O N

N o t e ▪ A small tonal change in the Chinese gives the word *Kwen* a double meaning: *contemplating* and *exhibiting*. Thus the hexagram refers both to the contemplator and the contemplated. All that is not one is the other; the hexagram is all-encompassing. The shape of the hexagram itself has an appropriately complementary meaning (as pointed out in the Richard Wilhelm translation) because its shape resembles a tower familiar in ancient China which, when situated on a mountain, could serve as a watchtower to those above and a landmark to those below. The shape of the hexagram, the shape of the tower, is also the shape of the Chinese symbol for Tao, the way: π. It is the gate of the eternal present between the future and the past, between the contemplator and the contemplated, as the man of the future surveys his past for meaningful, relevant experiences.

A r t h a ▪ You deal with the past and future in a balanced and consistent manner. You live fully in the present—not as a saint, free of the illusion of time, but able to keep the illusions of past and future in proper perspective. You do not rely too heavily on experience. Nor do you dwell in the past. You are always prepared for changes and the unexpected does not surprise you. You are aware of your direction and acknowledge certain goals and aspirations, but you view them realistically, knowing that reality ultimately never coincides with its ideal. Neither the past nor future is as sacred to you as the present. You move freely, not blocked by the idea of time. You resemble the symbol derived from the trigrams, the wind blowing above the earth. You are a traveler—but neither on a quest nor on the run. You travel because you are not attached to static precedents, or stymied by fears, or limited by cumbersome strategies. If you do not travel geographically, you travel in the sense of moving on from experience to experience. As an ideal example to those more involved with the karma of past and future, your balanced character is a good influence.

K a m a ▪ You have a well-balanced relationship with Friend. Selfish and unselfish, domineering and docile, aggressive and passive impulses stir you—and you see all such impulses clearly, in their proper perspective. The result, from Friend's point of view, is that you are wonderfully responsive, both in gratifying Friend's needs and in gratifying Friend's need to gratify you.

M o k s h a ▪ It is in your Tao to be enlightened by contemplating the meaning of this hexagram.

L I N E S

1. — x — He looks at things
          like a barefoot boy.

*No blame
if you are small;
if you are great
you will regret it.*

Your balanced contemplation of the past and future is somewhat obscured by an element of fantasy which you project in both directions. If you are in a position where you must set an example for others, this element of fantasy can be troublesome and harmful. Otherwise it is of slight importance.

2. — x — She peeps out from behind the door.
*Keep to your course
if you are Yin.*

You have a balanced view of the past and future, but it is narrow and limited as well. If you are content with a circumscribed and simple life, there is no harm in this. If you have taken on a broader and fuller, more active way of life, this narrowness will be a drawback.

3. — x — He examines his own life
and chooses advance or retreat accordingly.

Step outside yourself and look at your life. Examine your past existence objectively, as an innocent stranger would; examine your ideals and aspirations as an objective expert consultant would. Then you will come to the right decision.

4. — x — He examines the lessons of politics.
He should try to get to know the ruler.

Your balanced view of the past and the future has given you special insights into the social processes. With this talent you should attempt to place yourself in an influential social or political position.

5. — o — He examines his own life.
No mistakes.

Your thoughts are inner-directed. You see the past and future in balance, but only as reflections of yourself. For a man without illusions and aware of his own absurdity, this is all right. For a man without a sense of humor, who retains illusions about himself, this is very bad. It makes his reality dangerously irrelevant to the day-to-day world about him.

6. ——o—— He contemplates his character
              and judges himself.
              No mistakes.

Your thoughts are outer-directed. You see the past and future in balance, but as distant, unreal archetypes, like works of art or emanations from a distant God—wholly unrelated to yourself. You do not take into account the extent to which you have been influenced by the past. You do not recognize your function as a source of what will occur in the future. For a man without illusions and aware of his own absurdity, this is all right. For a man without a sense of humor, who retains illusions about himself, this is very bad. It makes his reality dangerously irrelevant to the day-to-day world about him.

21

Shih-Ho · Biting Through

 Thunder
below

 The Sun
above

O R A C L E

The teeth of the lightning illuminate
the majesty of the thunder.
By fitting the penalties to the crime
the ancient kings illuminated their laws.

Success.
Follow the legally prescribed course.

I N T E R P R E T A T I O N

A r t h a ▪ Someone is doing you an injustice. Someone is
acting dishonestly toward you; perhaps even criminally. It could
be anything from a hypocritical deception in an important personal relationship to fraud perpetrated on you as buyer or seller
or even to illegal discrimination against you by a government
authority. You must take advantage of the rule of law, the protec-
tion incorporated into our leviathan social system. If it is war-
ranted, bring criminal action against whomever or whatever is
inhibiting your legal rights. If the dishonesty is on a more personal level you must break off the relationship firmly. Be careful,
however, not to act out of a spirit of revenge; don't get carried
away. Whatever you do, do openly, either according to the letter
of the law or according to your own principles of behavior. When

laws are vague and their execution is arbitrary, the fabric of society weakens and comes apart. In your personal life as well, if your own principles are vague you will be more likely to tolerate a basically uncongenial and unsuitable situation.

K a m a ▪ You or Friend or a third party is knowingly behaving dishonestly toward the other(s), causing unhappiness and grief. If it is you, you must cease immediately; if you cannot treat Friend with candor, then break off the relationship. If it is Friend who is dishonest, you must discover what the deception is and confront Friend with it. Unless Friend responds with frankness and love you must break off the relationship. If it is a third party, his dishonesty toward you and/or Friend is a conscious effort to destroy your relationship.

M o k s h a ▪ What you see of your spiritual life is a veil, a mask. Someone—and it could be you, yourself—is deluding you about the nature of your spiritual course. You may think of yourself as being in a close union with the One and All, when in actuality a basic dishonesty has fettered you to the wheel of karma. You could be deceiving yourself by piously rationalizing a compulsive addiction to a drug, to licentiousness, or to acquisitiveness. The deception could be your mistaking a selfish, subjective attachment for a response to divine charisma. Or rituals that have become habitual may be undermining your efforts at transcendence.

L I N E S

1. ——o—— His feet are in the stocks;
        he loses his toes.
        No mistakes.

The dishonesty being perpetrated on you has not yet gone far enough to be serious and irreversible. If you act now, reconciliation is possible.

2. — x — The man bites through soft meat;
he loses his nose.
No mistakes.

The wrong being done to you is so blatant and unmitigated that
you are liable to overreact and come down very, very hard on the
offenders. Your anger is justified.

3. — x — The man bites through dry meat;
he encounters something rotten.
A few minor regrets.
No major mistakes.

Time is essential. You cannot afford the time demanded by the
usual channels. You have assumed more authority than you really
have. At the showdown you will be powerless and embarrassed.
You will not be blamed, though; the nature of the emergency
makes your actions acceptable.

4. — o — The man bites through dry meat
stuck to the bone.
Money and weapons are pledged to him.
Auspicious
if you keep to your course
and recognize the difficulties.

Your tormentor has immense power. Be hard as nails, persistent,
and on your guard; in the end, you will overcome.

5. — x — The man bites through dry meat;
he encounters gold.
Keep to your course,
recognizing your peril.
No mistakes.

You have a gentle nature and incline to be lenient toward wrong-
doers. If by the rule of law or according to your own principles
certain harsh actions must be taken, do not let your forgiving
nature dissuade you. Not fully using the law, in a legal action,
undermines the fabric of society; stretching your principles, in
more personal matters, undermines the fabric of your life. By

assuming a role in society and assuming a personal ethos you
have assumed contingent responsibilities.

6. ——o—— The man wears a yoke;
         he loses his ears.
         Ominous.

Whoever the offender is, he is incorrigible and intractable. It
could be yourself.

22

Pee ▪ Beauty

The Sun
below

The Mountain
above

O R A C L E

A fire burns at the foot of the mountain.
The superior man is brilliant as an administrator
but he does not dare act as a judge.

Keep to your course
but do not let it overwhelm you.

I N T E R P R E T A T I O N

A r t h a ▪ You are an artist. You have the ability to discover and delineate forms and patterns that have a universal
meaning. Your work communicates with others through the commonly understood universality of its form—i.e., its beauty. Besides working artists, there are those whose lives are beautiful
in some way: they communicate to others through the transcendent quality, the universality, of some aspect of their lives.
The currently widely accepted view that the work of the artist is
synonymous with "self-expression" is a misleading anomaly. In
your work, in your day-to-day life, you may express your hopes,
your fears, your pride, your shame, your political views, your
psychological theories, a physical fact or the primacy of a certain
underarm deodorant and you may be more or less successful in
communicating this. However, as an artist, whatever you
express, communicated with varying degrees of success, is only

a medium for the beauty of the expression, which has little do with its personal meaning. There is something universal in what you express that communicates to others perfectly—clearly, directly, untransformed, and untransformable. The artist is proverbially misunderstood. Your art is not the content of your work or life, but its form. The beauty of Isadora Duncan, for example, is in what her life *was* and not its intent: her story communicates deeply—a graceful fluttering between joy and tragedy. A tintype of her in a dance pose, however, arouses twitters at least as often as awe and the dance theories and education theories that were the overwhelming effort of her life are unfamiliar to most people. You are to others something else other than what you intend. It may be that an activity of yours that seems to you to be ordinary, natural, thoughtless, easy, seems to others to be a prototype of the human condition and a reflection of universal truth: a work of art. Do not undertake any actions that you consider important or crucial. Such actions inevitably will be misunderstood by others. Do not hold back in small matters, though.

K a m a ▪ Your relationship with Friend is based on beauty you perceive in each other. There is a kind of intermediary between you, an aesthetic ether, that transforms what each of you are to yourselves into a symbol meaningful to the other. You worship Friend's physical form or enjoy the form of Friend's communication with you (as opposed to its content) or you delight in the form of your sexual congress or you thrill to the form of the tension between you; you don't worship, enjoy, delight in, or thrill to Friend. If this aesthetic appreciation is mutual and if the relationship remains on that plane, you will be a beautiful and tranquil couple. If the aesthetic appreciation is one-sided, then each of you will feel wronged and misunderstood.

M o k s h a ▪ "Confucius felt very uncomfortable when once, on consulting the oracle, he obtained the hexagram of grace." (*The I Ching*, trans. Wilhelm/Baynes.) Wilhelm goes on to suggest that the reason for Confucius's discomfort was the transitoriness of tranquillity. Rather, it was Confucius's realization that his teachings communicated not through the literal truth of his words, but through their form. His life communicated through its inner peace, not his actions. His teachings communicated through their sentiment and aptness, not through their meanings. The familial religious system he formulated communicated not through the divine inspiration he felt, but through the system's logic, order, and circumspection. Aesthetically inspired religious experiences as a rule don't carry over after the aesthetic experience is finished. It is the transitoriness of the beautiful revelation that caused Confucius's discomfort. If the example of Confucius does not apply to you, then the example of his followers does. What you consider to be a spiritual experience is essentially an aesthetic one. The experience can be the same; what differs is the source of your ecstatic reaction. It is the beauty of the ritual or the beauty of the expression of the teachings or the beauty of the mythology that moves you; not a single, radiant revelation of your chosen path. If you cannot recognize this, you are in danger of being eventually disillusioned.

L I N E S

1. ——o—— He decorates his feet.
   He can dismiss his carriage
   and walk.

It is the easy and natural quality of your life that is especially appreciated by other people. If you were to appear motivated and willful you would lose the goodwill of your friends and colleagues. Any desires, any hopes you have will naturally take shape if your life proceeds on its admirably effortless way.

2. —x— He trims his beard.

You think you realize what it is in you that others find aesthetically pleasing and you have tried to refine it, cultivate it. Naturally this disrupts its form, which so far has been pleasing because of its unforced, unconscious quality. Your self-consciousness imposes on your art or life changes which are personal, and meaningless to others. Vanity, vanity!

3. —•— He is elegant
         and is favored.
         Auspicious
         if you keep to your course.

You live a life of pleasure. If you accept it without grasping, without anxieties: good fortune, continued pleasure. If you devote yourself to sustaining it: misfortune and frustration.

4. —x— He is elegant, all in white.
         On a white winged horse
         he seeks union,
         sending before him
         not a robber, but a serious suitor.

The beauty you create endears you to others. You are valued by others. You have a certain brilliance that attracts social recognition. You know how to develop this quality and how to use your advantage for meaningful, unselfish ends. But now you feel hesitant. You feel that if you continue to pursue social success you may lose yourself, you may lose your freedom to make choices according to your own principles. The fact that you feel a doubt points to the validity of the doubt and also to its resolution: you must withdraw from your estimable social position into a life of simplicity and warmth, with fewer, closer friends with whom you share a deep communication and love.

5. —x— He is elegant among those
         who live on hills and have gardens.
         The roll of silk he bears is small and slight.
         Although you may appear to be stingy,
         auspicious
         in the end.

Disillusioned with your former milieu, revolted by its materialistic, selfish ideology, you are trying to break away and enter a new social sphere, a new circle, whose principles you find more sympathetic. Because you are still unfamiliar with the symbols and gestures of those you wish to join, you have difficulty making contact. But the basic empathy between yourself and those you seek to know will slowly draw you into their company.

6. —o— He wears only white.
   No mistakes.

There is no distinction between form and content in what you do. Like St. Francis's entire life or the swift answer to a koan by a monk in satori, the beauty of the form and the revelation of its content are identical. The basic element in such a cohesion is simplicity—a unity of thought and action. Artistic genius. Happiness.

23

Po · Collapse

The Earth
below

The Mountain
above

 O R A C L E

The mountain rests on the earth.
The superior man strengthens his support
in order to maintain his position.

Take no action whatsoever.

I N T E R P R E T A T I O N

A r t h a ▪ You are off balance. The predominant forces in
your life emanate from outside you, pressing on you from many
sides. They are earthbound, materialistic, self-perpetuating.
Whatever imaginative, spiritual, independent force you have
weakens daily. The image of the mountain on the earth symbolizes the proper response to your situation: absolute stillness. Go
nowhere; do nothing. If you can assist others in realizing their
own material goals, you can hold your own.

K a m a ▪ Discord caused by conflicting selfish desires has
brought you and Friend to the point of parting. Only if you quell
your emotions and your expectations is there any chance the
relationship will continue.

M o k s h a ▪ Your spiritual path is overgrown with weeds of bad karma. All your rituals, sacrifices, meditations, and "revelations" are infused with nonspiritual desires and materialistic ideals. Cease your spiritual practice. By ceasing your spiritual practice perhaps you can rid yourself of the selfish needs that are feeding on it . . . then again, perhaps not.

L I N E S

1. — x — The couch is overturned
        by hacking off its legs.
        Ominous.
        Destruction
        if you keep to your course.

If you move or act you will fall and become prey to the forces that are threatening to overwhelm you. If you take no action, as the oracle recommends, you will still be prey to these self-seeking forces, because you remain approachable and defenseless. You are damned if you do and damned if you don't.

2. — x — The couch is overturned
        by hacking its frame.
        Ominous.
        Destruction
        if you keep to your course.

You have tried to advance from the hopeless situation presented in the oracle of the moving first line. You have chosen to move slightly in order to avoid the threat. You have lost your balance and are about to fall.

3. — x — He is among those
        who overturn the couch.
        No mistakes.

You recognize the power of the forces threatening you, and compromise with them. Considering the extent of the difficulties you were in, there is no guilt in following this propitiatory course.

4. — x — He overturns the couch
   and bruises the man who was on it.
   Ominous.

Total defeat.

5. — x — He leads others along
   like fish on a line
   and obtains for them favors
   usually reserved for the royal household.
   Improvement
   in every way.

You act rapaciously and materialistically. Your character will improve as your fortunes do.

6. — o — He is like a large fruit
   still uneaten.
   The man finds the people
   who will carry him like a chariot.
   Smaller men overturn their own dwellings.

There is no finality in any situation. Even though you have been thrown off balance and the structure of your life has toppled, there is more to come. What happens next is the "fruit" of the oracle for this line. It is a "large fruit" because your downfall was extensive and much has been changed. Be responsive to the new. Do not founder on the ideals of the past. You can find in your own destruction a vehicle to carry you to a new life. If you retain the ideals and dreams of the past the only fruit of your disaster will be unhappiness.

24

Fiu ▪ Returning

Thunder
below

The Earth
above

O R A C L E

Thunder within the earth.
At the winter solstice,
the ancient kings closed the borders,
forced the merchants to rest
and the inspectors to take a holiday.
The man comes and goes freely;
he is not at fault.
In seven days he returns;
his friends come to greet him.

Improvement, whatever you do.

I N T E R P R E T A T I O N

N o t e ▪ The winter solstice was regarded by the ancient Chinese as a time of rest. The thunder of spring is still asleep beneath the cold earth. It is the very beginning of the yearly season of growth. It is the yearly turn for the better—imperceptible, natural, irreversible.

A r t h a ▪ You have passed the low point of a dormant, stagnating situation. Improvement will now come naturally, in the rhythm of the natural flux—just as the Yang line enters the hexagram in the lowest place, in harmony with the natural bottom-to-top movement of the lines. Along with other people, you are experiencing a change of fortune—a turn for the better that is occurring without anyone's having willed it, planned it, or arranged for it. It occurs completely on its own, in its own slow time, in its own quiet way. Very gradually you will find your life becoming more eventful. Because all the lines it approaches are receptive Yin lines, the entering Yang line meets no resistance as it moves upward. In the same way, the new forces that have entered your life, refreshingly different and more vital than previously, will cause no conflict, no strained relationships, no discomfort to anyone. They are unanimously welcomed. The widespread enthusiasm for this change will make acquaintances out of strangers and friends out of acquaintances. Do not try to accelerate this change. It must be allowed to develop in its own slow, deliberate manner. To try to force it would be as foolish as disturbing the frozen earth over dormant seeds.

K a m a ▪ This hexagram indicates a new force forming in an old relationship. In the natural course of time your relationship with Friend has become a mutually passive, unemotional one. Throughout this low-key period, throughout this stagnation of passion, you have remained relaxed, without anxiety: you have accepted the natural flow of your life. You have reached a point of such quiet, loving receptivity that you will respond naturally and healthily to this new and different blossoming of your love.

M o k s h a ▪ You have reached a turn for the better in your spiritual path. You sense it, although you cannot verbalize it or determine its source. Although it is obviously a new, fresh, unexplored direction, it proceeds directly from the path you presently follow. Let the rhythmic waves of change move in their own time. Do not plunge into a new course—you will only find yourself thrashing helplessly about. What will happen has begun to happen. You sense its starting; as it proceeds you will sense its progress. Meanwhile, remain yourself. Practice only what you fully understand. Let it happen. Let it be.

L I N E S

1. —⊖— Return after a slight mistake.
   Very auspicious.
   Without guilt.

You contemplate taking a course that is contrary to your deepest principles. Your thoughts have not yet been transformed into action. Banish unprincipled ideas immediately, before they obsess you to the point of forcing you to act on them. There is no need to feel guilty—yet.

2. —x— Proud return.
   Auspicious.

You sense new ideas in the air, a new atmosphere, a new excitement. You are almost at the point of accepting them and enjoying them. You have been won over gradually, as this creative force has slowly permeated society and gradually has touched and influenced people you know.

3. —x— Return again and again.
   Without guilt.
   Caution!

You have a tendency, when things are going well for you, to interrupt the flow of events and to turn away from it, negatively. When you have slipped back far enough you again reverse yourself and attempt to regain what you purposefully let go. This line is the line of self-defeatism—not in extremis, but the defeatism of constant backsliding, the defeatism of fear of climax, fear of completion, fear of attainment. You remain guiltless because the impulse does not stem from inhumane ideals and harms no one but yourself.

4. —x— He leaves among others
   yet returns on his own.

You have sensed a change, a regeneration, a turn for the better in your situation. Your friends and colleagues have not felt it yet.

Move with it freely and naturally, even though this will alienate you from others.

5. — × — Noble return.
           Without guilt.

You are the pivot of the changes taking place. As you move in the new direction—contrary to accepted, traditional ideas—everything and everyone will fall in behind you.

6. — × — Confusion over returning;
           he goes astray.
           If he chooses to be aggressive
           his defeat will be far-reaching.
           Its effect will be felt even after ten years.
           Ominous.
           Guilt.
           Calamities.

A turn for the better has come and gone. You have let it pass you by. Conservative and fearful, you have stuck to old, decayed ideas, a stagnant way of life, an outdated, outmoded routine. You believe you display backbone by resisting change; you mistake your fear for stubbornness. This attitude is disastrous. It denies the inevitable flow of change in the universe—a flow which will carry you along, if not buoyant and upright, then tumbled headlong and willy-nilly. But the moment has passed. You can do nothing about it now. You must patiently wait for things again to resolve themselves.

25

Wiu-Wang · The Simple

*Thunder
below*

*Heaven
above*

O R A C L E

Thunder rolls beneath heaven.
It is in its nature.
The ancient kings, in tune with nature,
took into account the changing seasons
when making regulations,
and nourished all things.

*Success
if you keep to your course.
Mistakes
if you have strayed from it;
do as little as possible.*

I N T E R P R E T A T I O N

A r t h a · Thunder rolls beneath heaven: simple action
and simple movement, in accord with the creative flux of the
universe. Free and harmonious human action is also simple—
free of motivation and expectation. You desire nothing, so whatever you receive is a blessing; you expect nothing so whatever
occurs is fresh and unexpected. To others, bogged down in strategy and theories, expectations and anxieties, whatever you do
seems brilliant and original. You are free of the limitations of
desire and experience. You react naturally, from an infinite range

of possible action. Your spontaneous, always "right" action will never fail to surprise those who act according to vague theories and neurotic expectations. Benign monarchs, such as the ancient kings of the oracle, are always refreshing surprises in a history crammed with tyrants, yet they do nothing more than naturally fulfill traditional ideals of the proper role of the ruler. It is possible, however, to be free of any conscious purpose, to seem—even to yourself—absolutely spontaneous and natural in your actions, and yet still not be in accord with the present moment and the present world. Actions that are purely instinctive but without a clear inner vision, without a direct, uninterrupted connection with the flow of the moment, can be disastrous and can cause misfortune to yourself and others. Compulsive actions, for example, seem to be spontaneous and unplanned, but they are not true responses to true situations, only pat responses triggered by prototype situations: symbolic action, not pertinent action. Habitual responses and activities, even if unconsciously based on the highest principles, are not enough involved with the present moment to be entirely successful and—especially for you who are not consciously aware that your way of responding is set and static—habitual activities often will have unfortunate results.

K a m a ▪ You are spontaneous and simple with Friend: or you *seem to be* spontaneous and simple. The presence of a quality of unexpectedness is a good test of the nature of your relationship with Friend. If your responses to Friend always seem new and direct, in the mood of the moment and in accord with Friend's feelings at the time, then you are fulfilling your Tao and your relationship will be a happy one. If your responses, no matter how considerate they may be or may seem, are predictable, then it is an indication that you are not fully in touch with Friend and with your entity as a living couple in the present moment. Such a subtle dishonesty will cause subtle conflicts.

M o k s h a ▪ The way of being simple in the Tao of this hexagram, as described in the first part of the "Dharma" section, indicates a perfect spiritual state. Very possibly it is a state of such simplicity that it comes from no particular spiritual path, uses none of the magic metaphors that are usually the means to the attainment of such a perfect state. But this hexagram does indicate a certain danger: the conscious cultivation of such simplicity. Your wise understanding of the freedom, the spontaneity and the simplicity that accompany the attainment of spiritual enlightenment may prompt you to emulate a state of divine spontaneity—not necessarily as a fraud, but perhaps as a sincere, but backward effort to attain Brahma. Someone who has attained perfect understanding, but not the perfect practice of it, may seem to others to be completely simple and "right" in the highest sense in whatever he does; to others his actions may seem always refreshing and unexpected. But someone who follows the way of simplicity without true spontaneity is not himself blind to this schism within him: beneath his benign exterior he still sorrows for the peace he cannot attain.

L I N E S

1. ——o—— The natural man acts naturally.
       Auspicious
       if you advance.

Trust your instincts.

2. —— x —— The natural man plows his field;
       not for the harvest to come,
       but just because it is time.
       The natural man cultivates his garden
       for three years;
       not for the greater beauty,
       but just because it is in the nature
       of gardens to be cultivated.
       Improvement
       no matter what you do.

If what you wish to undertake is a direct response to your present circumstances, then go ahead. If what you wish to do is an element in a strategy, if certain desired future results depend on it, then you had better not go ahead with it.

3. — x — A traveler steals an ox that has been tied
near the home of the natural man.
The natural man is accused and arrested.
Calamity.

In popular terms, what has befallen you is bad luck. Your simplicity makes such misfortune seem especially undeserved. You yourself accept such accidents philosophically. Free of expectations, you are free of disappointment. Free of motivation, you are free of regrets.

4. — o — *No mistakes*
if you keep to your course.

You are under pressure to act in a particular way, because in terms of other people's values and theories, such action seems called for in your situation. Retain the natural quality of your action and expression and do not allow what you do to be influenced in any way by outside pressures.

5. — o — The natural man falls ill.
He does not resort to medicine
and recovers naturally.

You have met with accidental misfortune, much graver than such events as simple material loss or social downgrading, which do not matter deeply to you. An illness. A sudden restriction from outside. Being victimized by gratuitous criminality. Etc. Although your level-headed, philosophical attitude may change to melancholy despair, do not give up your precious simplicity in your efforts to save yourself. If you worry and plot, you will do yourself more harm than good. Let nature take its course. Accept your situation as it is and react spontaneously and freely to it, without embellishing it with fantasies of dire and dreadful consequences.

6. — o — The natural man is sure to make a mistake
if he takes action.
No improvement.

Do not trust your instincts, do not trust any plans or expectations you may have. Keep from doing anything. Lie low.

26

Teh-Khiu · Major Restraint

Heaven
below

The Mountain
above

O R A C L E

Heaven within the mountain.
The superior man stores within his mind
the words and deeds of history,
in order to know what is right.

Keep to your course.
Do not hoard your rewards.
Do not begrudge your debt to society.
You may cross the great water.

I N T E R P R E T A T I O N

A r t h a · Your influence on others is strong and direct. You
have a real, overt and authorized control over many events in the
lives of many people. You have status, you have trust, you have
influential friends, and—if you are typically corrupt—you have
power. You achieved your position legitimately, through honest
dealings, good works, and fairness. Because of your position you
have the means to lead an extremely leisurely, comfortable life.
But you must accept the responsibilities that accrue and daily enter vigorously into the world of men and affairs, bringing to them
the influence of your principles. The danger of this course is habit.
Habitual activity for someone in your position becomes more and
more ineffectual as time passes. You must spend your time doing

what needs most to be done, changing your sphere of activity with changing circumstances, always reacting directly and pertinently to change. Any important and far-reaching steps you wish to take at this time will meet with success.

K a m a ▪ With Friend's love and consent you have absolute control over your relationship. Friend accedes to you in everything without question and without resentment. Thus, you also have complete responsibility as well. There is a danger that you will find a comfortable groove and settle habitually into it. You must always be responsive to Friend's and your own changing circumstances and needs.

M o k s h a ▪ Turn to the ancient sources of whatever spiritual path you have chosen. Through all the maya of vague words and outdated concepts and all the contradictions of the past will come revelations that will open your mind and liberate you.

L I N E S

1. ——o—— *Halt!*
    You are in peril.

You must suppress your strong impulse to act immediately and vigorously. You see the obstacle that confronts you. If you recognize its strength you understand that you must halt. You must hold yourself back, frustrated but still undefeated. Take advantage of any opportunities that arise for the release of your pent-up energies.

2. ——o—— The strap that holds back the carriage
    has been removed.

You find yourself opposed by a power and an influence greater than your own. Submit. Remain aware of changes in the balance of forces and be ready to act as soon as the balance is in your favor.

3. —⊖— He has good horses and drives himself on.
   Keep to your course,
   recognizing the difficulties involved.
   Train daily to defend yourself against them.
   You may advance
   in any direction.

You have made contact with others of influence who have the same principles and direction as yourself. Act in concord with them. There is still danger from certain obstacles, so you must remain on your guard. While being sincere with those you have joined for common action toward a common goal, you must remain alertly and suspiciously on your guard against potential opposition. You should arrange for emergency contingencies and keep in mind a possible sanctuary in case your opposition overwhelms you.

4. —×— A piece of wood has been placed
   on the young bull's head
   where his horns will be.
   Very auspicious.

If a block of wood is affixed to a young bull's head, his horns will be rendered harmless. If you possess comparable foresight you can take simple and painless effective action immediately to eliminate once and for all the forces that threaten you.

5. —×— The tusks of a castrated boar.
   Auspicious.

The tusks of a boar are always dangerous. But if the boar is castrated he no longer has the propensity to use them. Although you cannot eliminate the power and danger of the forces that threaten you, by taking effective action now you can change their essential natures from threatening to something more benign.

6. —⊖— The man commands the firmament.
   Success.

You have achieved great success, you have great influence and occupy a lofty position in the world. You have, in fact, achieved everything you have wished.

27

Ih ▪ Nourishment

*Thunder
below*

*The Mountain
above*

O R A C L E

Thunder within the mountain
explodes from the volcano.
The superior man controls his mouth;
what comes out of it
and what he puts into it.

*Auspicious
if you keep to your course.
Thoughtfully consider
what it is you wish to nourish;
thoughtfully consider
what will best nourish it.*

I N T E R P R E T A T I O N

A r t h a ▪ The meaning of this hexagram is echoed by
Norman O. Brown's "We are what we eat." And so we are—be it
wurst or Ten Happiness Mandarin Suckling Pig or organic foods,
naturally prepared. This is the hexagram of eating properly.
Watch the cycle of nourishment from earth to plants, plants to
animals, and from animals back to earth again. Feel its texture.
Smell its odors. Notice its colors. See what is used and what is
discarded. Keeping in mind that you, too—intellectual, spiritual, divine though you may be—are an animal, a part of this

great cycle, you will instinctively know what you should eat for nourishment and you will desist from eating the kind of food that serves only to quell cravings or excite your palate. The interpreters of the I Ching could never have imagined how far man would wander from the source of his food. Unless you are very unusual whatever you do in order to obtain nourishment is quite unconnected with that nourishment itself. The providing of nourishment for oneself has become a commercial transaction between consumer and merchant—no longer a communion with the earth. The life-sustaining property of food is forgotten; food is just another economic success symbol. Food seems to come from nowhere and to have been grown by no one. Respect your food as you respect yourself; treat it as you treat yourself. You are what you eat. You cannot fulfill your direction, you cannot follow your Tao, if you do not naturally follow your course in the life cycle of the earth.

K a m a ▪ You may have achieved a deep state of warmth, understanding, and stability with Friend. But you neglect your physical needs in favor of illusionary concepts and ideas of love; you neglect the essence of your relationship. It is, after all, a relationship between two whole people, not two minds. You must become as unselfish and loving with your body as you are generous and sympathetic with your mind.

M o k s h a ▪ Your path to enlightenment calls for an ascetic life. You must eat the simplest foods in small quantities, enough to provide you with health and strength, but not for pleasure or out of habit. In the same way that you have discarded nonessential words and thoughts, you must dispose of your nonessential flesh. If a regimen does not naturally occur to you, find a given diet with a philosophical basis within an organized religious sect or congregation.[1]

[1] The popular macrobiotic diet intends to balance the Yin and Yang within the body. It is a recently developed discipline, unknown to the ancients. The diet's staple is brown rice.

L I N E S

1. —o— "You ignore the example of the tortoise
         and look at me with a long face."
         Ominous.

(Tortoiseshell markings were the original source of the patterns
of Yin and Yang that form the hexagrams of the oracles.) You
have everything you need, yet are filled with resentment. You
envy those who have encumbered their lives with more than
you have. These absurd covetous values are so important to you
that they color your entire life, to the extent that you consult the
I Ching about them.

2. —x— The man seeks nourishment from below;
         unworthy.
         If the man seeks nourishment from above
         he will be involved in trouble.

You are able to provide nourishment for yourself, yet you continue to accept it from other sources.

3. —x— The man's actions
         inhibit proper nourishment.
         Ominous
         even if you keep to your course.
         Do not take any action
         for ten years.

You completely neglect the needs of your body. You have no real
sense of your physical self. There can be no situation that war-
rants such neglect. Everything you do is affected by it.

4. —x— The man seeks to provide for those below.
         Like a tiger glaring down from a tree
         he is ready to spring.
         Auspicious.
         No mistakes.

You have a strong desire to provide yourself with the essentials of
life. This is a natural desire, not based on sensual cravings or the

seeking of social position. If you are alert to favorable circumstances and aggressive in taking advantage of them, you are only following a natural bent and there is no guilt or wrongdoing involved in it.

5. —x— The man acts unconventionally.
   Auspicious
   if you keep to your course.
   Do not cross the great water.

Your concern with proper nourishment is somewhat extreme. Your diet has assumed too great a role in your life. Try to bring your values more into proportion. Do not attempt any major undertakings.

6. —x— The man is the source of nourishment.
   Auspicious
   but perilous.
   You may cross the great water.

You are aware that the source of all nourishment is the One and All. You accept what you have and desire nothing. As long as you do not separate your animal instincts from your transcendental ones—as long as you do not starve yourself—things will go well for you and you can take any major steps you wish.

28

The Wind
below

The Marsh
above

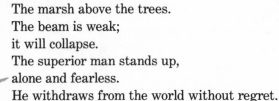

O R A C L E

The marsh above the trees.
The beam is weak;
it will collapse.
The superior man stands up,
alone and fearless.
He withdraws from the world without regret.

Success
if you take action
in any direction.

I N T E R P R E T A T I O N

A r t h a ▪ Watch out! The roof is about to cave in. The trigram The Marsh, above Wind/Wood, suggests an unnatural weight. The most serious matters of your life have all overtaken you at the same time. Everything seems to be happening at once. Unusually strong pressures from outside bear down on you. There is no way of holding off any one situation until the others are resolved—they are all coming to a head now. The times are momentous, threatening, desperate. Your problems cannot be solved—but you need not let them crush you. The tree survives the flood by standing straight beneath the floodwaters. It does not give with the water, it does not bend familiarly to accommodate it, like the reeds and grasses. It meets the water head-on, taking it in all its force, as it is obscured beneath the waves. The tree outlasts the flood; the tree remains essentially tree, while the water, by rising, denies its own nature, which is to seek its own level. You cannot avoid troubles, but if you remain confident you will come through unscathed.

K a m a ▪ You have too many emotional ties, too many love relationships happening at the same time. All at once you have gotten yourself involved in a number of demanding close situations—and you cannot handle them. All your separate affairs are about to overlap and erupt. You should attempt, without anxiety or pride and with patience, to extricate yourself from all of them. You cannot resolve anything, you cannot please anyone or forestall the forthcoming conflicts and outbursts, but you can—if it is not too late—withdraw from the whole thing. It requires a spirit of resignation, bolstered by self-reliance and self-esteem.

M o k s h a ▪ You are in a spiritual crisis. You are in anguish over many contradictory impulses. They are pulling you apart. You are filled with numerous strong beliefs that seem to cancel out one another, making all seem meaningless. Your path is blocked. You must drop all your conflicting beliefs, forget your so-called understanding, dispense with any traditional, ritualistic practices. Like the tree in the flood, you must stand alone in the flood of karma, alone, without metaphysics, among the illusions of sky and furniture. If you can renounce all the heavy, soul-searing, mind-expanding revelations you have had and stand physically in the world, by yourself, without them, the attainment of enlightenment will be infinitely closer than it is now.

L I N E S

1. — x — The man places mats of white grass
             beneath objects set on the ground.
             No mistakes.

You should take extraordinary precautions, for these are potentially dangerous times. Although in being so careful you may inconvenience some people and meet with incredulity and aggression, you are actually doing the best thing for yourself and for everyone else concerned.

2. ——o—— A rotting willow produces shoots.
　　　　　The old man possesses his young wife.
　　　　　General improvement.

Rejuvenation: untimely, unexpected success in business; or a rejuvenation of passion and love; or a renaissance of your most profound spiritual revelations. Do whatever you wish.

3. ——o—— The beam is weak.
　　　　　Ominous.

You do not heed the warnings of others; you do not heed the clear signs of ruptures and destruction ahead; you will not believe the oracle of the I Ching. The consequences of your stubbornness will be unfortunate.

4. ——o—— The beam is braced.
　　　　　Auspicious.
　　　　　If you look for more support
　　　　　you will regret it.

Someone has come to your aid. The dangers of your situation have been mitigated through his efforts. Now you can handle things successfully. Danger: do not try to take advantage of your benefactor's brotherly affection by insinuating further demands on him.

5. ——o—— Flowers sprout from a rotting willow.
　　　　　The old woman possesses her young husband.
　　　　　No blame.
　　　　　No praise.

Flowers blossom on a dead tree; an old woman makes love. But flowers do not regenerate the tree, nor does a husband regenerate an old woman. Signs of vigor and springlike energy have entered your life. But they will not change your life, which remains repressed beneath the weight of your own essential nature.

6. — × — The man walks straight into the stream
and keeps right on going
until he finally disappears beneath the water.
Ominous
but no blame.

Blindly you have walked right into disaster. You could have avoided it, but your mind was on other things. Stand up to it the best you can, although you are helpless in a hopeless situation. At least comfort yourself with the realization that you have wronged no one but yourself and have perpetrated no evil.

29

The Deep
below

The Deep
above

O R A C L E

The deep within the deep.
The superior man is a teacher
and practices what he preaches.
Because of his sincerity
He is said to have a penetrating mind.

Any action
is valuable.

I N T E R P R E T A T I O N

A r t h a ▪ The trigram *K'an*, the Deep, represents danger. The hexagram *Khan* indicates repeated danger: danger as a
way of life. You are at your best when your life is fraught with
danger. You choose your course and find your strength in reacting to the dangers that beset you; without them you would be
indecisive and lax. Since you are most effective when under
pressure, the dangerous elements of a situation enhance it for
you. Since this predilection for danger fosters excitement, a
sense of challenge, and an acute awareness and not anxiety,
defeatism, and indecision, it is a positive, creative force. If it is
accompanied by a compatibility between your principles and
your activity, you can successfully avoid trouble.

K a m a ▪ You constantly bring your relationship to a crisis state in order to renew and revive your love for Friend. Without the threat of an imminent breaking up of the relationship you cannot remain sufficiently emotionally involved for it to hold together. You repeatedly put your own love and Friend's to the test. The more difficult and dangerous the test, the more you feel, the more you desire, the more you love. Unless Friend's psychology comfortably fits in with your system of repeated crises you will face crises and conflicts *not* of your own making— less titillating and more extreme than those you yourself compulsively create.

M o k s h a ▪ Your spiritual practice is based on the constant presence of death. You achieve your spiritual revelations, your religious experiences, by confronting death—not abstractly and philosophically, but directly, bodily, in time and space. It is likely that your first important spiritual experience occurred while you were in grave physical danger—in grave illness or in a nearly fatal mishap or in battle. The spiritual experience of a confrontation with death is not necessarily tantamount in the lives of such daredevils as racing drivers, sky divers, and mercenary adventurers. But in *your* case it *is* the quest for such enlightening confrontations, your deep need for them—perhaps a kind of addiction to them—that impels you into constant danger. A confrontation with death is a confrontation with the Infinite—a brilliant, cleansing, enlightening experience. Hemingway was a well-known practitioner of the adventurous moksha.

L I N E S

1. — x — Already beneath the deep,
          he stumbles into a chasm.
          Ominous.

You have lived with danger for too long. You have become callous. The presence of danger no longer heightens your awareness, keeps you on your guard, or gives you the sense of purpose to sufficiently protect yourself. You cannot undermine danger simply by being blasé.

2. —⊘— All the dangers of the deep confront him.
        Some relief.

The dangers you face are real and powerful. You should confine your activities to whatever few small endeavors you have well under control.

3. —x— The depths confront him on every hand.
        Everything is dangerous; he is never at rest.
        His struggles will plunge him
        into the chasm within the deep.
        Take no action.

You have gotten yourself into a position where your reaction to danger will only plunge you into other grave and unknown dangers. No matter how distasteful and precarious inaction may seem, you must not act now. Let things take their course and do not try either to avoid or overcome whatever threatens you.

4. —x— The man is at a feast:
        just wine in a clay cup
        and rice in a clay bowl.
        He matches his lessons
        to the intelligence of his host.
        *No mistakes
        in the end.*

You have found a haven from the dangers that beset you. It is a humble place, far below your expectations, where you are not able to use your full talents. Although your potential may remain unfulfilled, you can fulfill yourself in this limited situation by giving of yourself totally to your benefactors in whatever ways can be understood, accepted and utilized by those who have kindly provided you with your humble shelter.

5. —⊘— The waters of the deep almost overflow.
        Order must be brought about.
        No mistakes.

The dangers that you face are grave and numerous. Concentrate exclusively on overcoming them. Do not do anything more than simply to protect yourself from present dangers. Do not attempt any new activities. Do not take on any new responsibilities. Do not get involved in any situations other than those with which you are involved now. In order to react effectively to the danger you face, your powers are already taxed to their maximum. Any new activity will cause you to overreach yourself.

6. — x —   He is bound with a heavy rope
                and thrown into a thicket of thorns.
                For three years he does not see the way out.
                Ominous.

All your troubles have come to a head. The time is not propitious. The dangers that beset you are too much for you to handle. You are trapped and at their mercy. Extended—but not permanent—bad luck.

30

Lee ▪ Fire

The Sun
below

The Sun
above

O R A C L E

Fire on fire.
The superior man refines his brilliance;
his light can be seen from near and far.

Be firm.
Success
without obstruction.
Auspicious
if you cultivate your docility.

I N T E R P R E T A T I O N

A r t h a ▪ Like fire, you give light and warmth; like fire, you must cleave to something in order to maintain your existence. You are bright, active, outgoing; but you must hold to something dark and passive for your sustenance. Light, warmth, and its heavenward direction constitute one aspect of fire; its other aspect is its dependence on the dark dead fuel to which it clings. It is this less spectacular side of your nature that you should cultivate. Although in human terms flames are the most striking element in any fire, from the fire's point of view, its fuel, that which sustains it, is the crucial element. Fire is dependent on its dark partner for its existence; it takes its form entirely from the form and nature of its fuel. You command the respect and attention of your associates, but you are completely dependent on the principles and inspiration of someone else who commands no public interest or admiration. Do not let your own brightness blind you to the essential dependence and docility of your nature.

K a m a ▪ *Your* character, *your* emotions, *your* ideas, *your* desires dominate your relationship with Friend. To an outsider it seems that Friend is dependent on you. Between you and Friend, you know that *Friend* is the molder of *your* character, the fuel for your emotions and the source of your ideas and desires. There is no need for you to correct the views of others as long as you acknowledge to yourself Friend's essential role in the relationship and accept Friend's dominion gratefully.

M o k s h a ▪ The trigram *Li* indicates the sun's movement in the course of a day. Doubled, as it is in this hexagram, it indicates the sun's repeated movement from day to day. Your spiritual practice must be a daily ritual. You are a source of light to others. To be truly in your Tao you should be regular and persistent in your spiritual practice.

L I N E S

(In this hexagram, the first three lines—the *Li* trigram— represents the sun's course in a day. The last three lines—again the *Li* trigram—represent three different degrees of fire.)

1. ──o── His steps are unsure
        but he moves with reverence.
        No mistakes.

The morning sun. It is a time of haste and business, and—in your case—confusion. Unsure steps indicate inefficiency and wasted time. But as long as your intentions remain unconfused and consistent, you do nothing wrong or evil.

2. — x — Yellow.
   Very auspicious.

The midday sun. Yellow symbolizes balance and harmony; it is the color of the golden mean. The sun is poised between morning and afternoon. All is right with the world. Everything goes well.

3. — ᵒ — The setting sun.
   The old man should beat on his pot and sing.
   Instead, he worries about death.
   Ominous.

The afternoon sun. It brings thoughts of mortality and consequent melancholy. When the great man's wife died, his friends came to visit and mourn with him. They found him sitting in front of his home, beating on a wine jug and singing. They were shocked. The great man replied, "My wife has entered the realm of eternity. I sit and beat my pot and sing. What harm is there in that?"

4. — ᵒ — He comes, on fire,
   flares up, dies and is forgotten.

The flare: a flame that burns brightly, but briefly, dying quickly. It burns with too much force. To sustain its brilliance its fuel is quickly used up. You waste your resources.

5. — x — Tears flow in torrents.
   Lamentation.
   Auspicious.

The holocaust: a fire out of control. Although not willfully, you cause hardship and worry for others. However, you should not desist in your unhindered efforts to transform the world.

6. — ᵒ — The man is sent as an agent of punishment.
   Wisely, he crushes the chiefs.
   He humanely discriminates between
   the evil men and the good men
   who have been duped.
   No mistakes.

The torch: a flame under control and useful to others. You are obeisant to the selfish and often violent aims of others. Do only what is necessary to achieve the aims of your masters. Do not destroy simply because you have been given the license to. The guilt that applies to those who use you need not fall on you.

31

H-Syen ▪ Tension

Mountain
below

The Marsh
Mist above

O R A C L E

The pond is cradled by the mountain.
The superior man feels calm and chivalrous.

*Success
if you keep to your course
and remain receptive to others.*

I N T E R P R E T A T I O N

A r t h a ▪ You alone have the ability to act, therefore you
hold all the power. You must act. But your action should be to
subordinate yourself and your power of action to the needs of
those who cannot act. This assumes that both you and the others
involved in this situation have a common bond of identical principles or goals. If the underlying motive behind your helpful attitude is a willful desire for an improved and even more powerful
position in the group or community, then problems and conflicts
will ensue.

K a m a ▪ The passive submits to the active; at the same
time, the active subordinates its activity to the passive. This is
the basic, primary social contract between man and woman. The
family was the first social unit. Man could sleep alone, hunt alone,

sing alone, and die alone—but he could not reproduce alone. Sexual union implied a mutual subjugation to a common ideal— the sexual union itself. Neither partner could do it alone and, therefore, they had to divide the responsibility between them: the male was responsible for acting, the female was responsible for being acted upon. These responsibilities carried over into the broader ideal of the couple. The male was responsible for acting on behalf of the female; the female was responsible for inaction on behalf of the male. When the family numbered more than two the situation necessarily became more complex. However, in most cultures the family relationship, no matter how complex—in a few the male and female roles are reversed—is the most stable, respected, and accepted social institution in the culture. This was so much so in China, for example, that the Taoists—very aware of the transitoriness of most social principles and ideals— saw the family relationship as one of the basic unalterable principles and used it to exemplify and differentiate between the eternal Yin and Yang. Although the roles and relationships were complex, with different family members responsible for action or inaction in certain defined situations, the family structure was understood and accepted by all. The religious depth and inspiration of Confucius could only be felt by a people to whom principles of familial relationships were as unalterable as the points of the compass. In our own culture, especially in the United States, the family relationship has completely broken down. Not only is the traditional family relationship not accepted, it is almost universally not even known or understood. No traditional division of roles and responsibilities in the family exists for most married couples. Most of the hopeless, insoluble problems in our culture are conflicts between family members, while in most other cultures the family structure is well defined; whatever conflicts do arise among family members can always be resolved relatively easily through application of commonly accepted principles. The following dialogue probably rings a familiar bell: it is a prototype of the confusion that exists between you and Friend. Man and woman are considering whether to do something or go somewhere together. Man: "What would you like to do?" Woman: "It's entirely up to you." Man: "It makes no difference to me. I'll do whatever you want to do." Woman: "Uh . . . uh . . . uh . . ." (expressing painful confusion). At the outset the man assumes a masculine, active role and takes the initiative. With his words he seems to subordinate his power to the needs of the woman. He feels he is being chivalrous. (In actuality, he is too confused about his role to assume the initiative in a constructive way.) What the man has really done is to unload his responsibility for decision onto the woman. She ducks out by assuming a traditionally passive role. So far, the man has spoken according to principles of courtship and chivalry and the woman has spoken according to principles of male domination. These principles conflict. By saying "It makes no difference to me," the man accepts the role of lord and master proffered him by the woman's deference (*her* sloughing off of the responsibility). Now he moves forward in French history from the age of chivalry to Versailles and its noblesse oblige. He successfully parries the initiative filled with feelings of patronizing charity. They have tossed this responsibility back and forth like a hot potato. Such exchanges can continue through many phrases and courtesies culled from various mutually accepted ideals of social relationships until one of the partners is stumped and dissolves in total confusion. Whoever is stumped first accepts the blame for not making the decision and, as a punishment, relinquishes his desires in the matter to the other. For, in almost every case, each of them *has* a definite idea of what he or she would like to do. The problem is that there is no common, traditional, unspoken rule as to whose will prevails in this matter. The common acceptance of common principles of behavior by you and Friend will help end the conflicts between you. Since, unfortunately, there are no unspoken principles that you each accept unconditionally and continually, you must confer and frame your own, intellectually and verbally. You and Friend must together make the contract that has been denied you by the confusion of values and relationships that plagues our culture. You must decide together under what circumstances you are to take the initiative and when you defer the initiative to Friend. When you are called on to take the initiative you must abolish all anxieties about your responsibility for the outcome of your action—anxieties induced by the empirical framework of our culture—and accept the responsibility, not for the outcome—which is not preordained and can never be foreseen—but for the action itself at the moment you take it. You must trust the compact made between you and Friend as the ancient Chinese trusted so explicitly their well-ordered and unquestionable tradition of the family relationship. Although this hexagram was very cut-and-dried to the ancient Chinese, the accomplishment of its Tao for the modern Westerner is one of his most difficult, exasperating, and lonely problems.

M o k s h a ▪ You must subordinate your life to your spiritual practice. As things stand now, you abuse the spiritual revelations you have experienced. You use them for comfort, for power, or for love without allowing them to influence you deeply, to change you. In order to unite with the One and All in enlightenment you must *give yourself* in all your human acts of decision, will and desire as completely as you *accept* the divine gifts of freedom, acceptance, joy, and creativity.

L I N E S

1. — x — Wiggling the big toe.

You are willing to make some changes in yourself in order to improve your situation. But the changes you will allow are so minor and insignificant that they will not noticeably affect the situation, which is very complex and requires a greater effort, a greater revolution in yourself, than you are willing to give.

2. — x — Flexing the calves.
   Ominous
   unless you stand still.

You wish to change, but you do not have any principles that you trust enough to use as guidelines for a new way of being. If you act now, precipitously: failure. If you subdue all your active impulses and wait quietly for things to develop, wait until you can make a congenial and acceptable change: success.

3. —o— Flexing the thighs,
          impatiently waiting in line.
          If you continue
          you will regret it.

You base your actions on principles of future rewards instead of
basing them on principles of present needs. But the future is an
illusion. It exists right now, as much as it ever will, in your own
mind. It will never reappear in any form. In the here and now
your actions are disordered and confused, their only frame of
reference being the fantasies of your expectations.

4. —o— Twitching all over.
          Only people who know the man
          are influenced by him.
          Auspicious
          if you keep to your course.
          No guilt.

The deepest motivations of your heart are based on universal
principles; if you were to follow them you would follow your Tao
perfectly. But you do not trust your deepest motivations. You are
convinced that you should be looking after yourself in a more
immediate, meaner fashion and attempting to influence people
and events in your favor. Although in a limited sense these
attempts are successful, by ignoring your deeper impulses you
have made the wheel of karma into a treadmill.

5. —o— The back is rigid.
          No guilt.

You have the power to act. And you have a strong will. Your will
binds everyone together; your actions are accepted by all. Your
power is legitimate.

6. —x— The tongue wags.

You are very strong when it comes to expressing principles of
purposeful action; but when it comes to acting purposefully, you
are weak. Nothing good will come of it; nothing bad will come
of it.

32

Heng  · Continuity

The Wind
below

Thunder
above

O R A C L E

Wind and thunder,
faithful always.
The superior man remains firm
and does not change his method.

Success
and no mistakes
if you keep to your course.
You may take any action you wish.

I N T E R P R E T A T I O N

N o t e ▪ This hexagram expresses the continuity of experience, the bridge between moment and moment that makes the universal flux comprehensible to us. Shiva is sometimes referred to as "the destroyer" because in his dance, in his perpetual motion—which is the universal flux—no instant is allowed to linger and each successive instant can be thought of as the destroyer of the previous one. Vishnu is sometimes referred to as "the creator" because it is through his three great strides through time and space that the relationships between individual instants are established. The instants perpetually created and destroyed by Shiva are brought together in a cohesive whole. The continu-

ity of ever-changing experience, the gift of Vishnu, is the subject
of this hexagram.

A r t h a ▪ If you wish your individuality to have meaning
for others—if you wish it to be recognizable, identifiable, commu-
nicable, then your identity must have continuity. You exist not
only as a physical being, but also as the sum of your actions and
the values they express, as a reflection of your motivating principles. These aspects of you must be as consistent as your physical
aspect. This is not to say that you must not change. Your body is
always changing, each successive state in physical change flow-
ing naturally from the preceding state into the next. Your actions
should flow one from the other naturally, moving in a single
direction, motivated by a single force. Do not stray from your set
course. Do not allow yourself to be sidetracked by things that
incidentally catch your attention. Do not jump from one thing to
another. Such breaks in your continuity would cause conflicts
with those who count on you to be consistent. If you have continuity in the total sense your relationship will be harmonious. Your
changes will relate to the changes of others. There will be no
mistake about who you are, so potential hostilities can be avoided
at the very beginning. Continuity does not imply conservatism—
on the contrary, it is the quality of moving with the times.

K a m a ▪ This hexagram represents the institution of marriage. Ideally, the married couple has the same need for continuity that the individual has. The bases of the couple's words and
actions in relation to each other are consistent, not the result of
whims. The husband and wife are totally predictable to each
other, totally familiar. Friend requires such a familiarity in order
to relate to you openly, without unexpressed reservations.
Friend's love is based on the continuity of all your qualities—not
just your physical constancy.

M o k s h a ▪ Your spiritual life must have continuity. Instead of taking ten steps on each of ten different paths, take a
hundred steps on one. An enlightened man is one who has become

complete. Only with continuity, with a consistent vision of the One and All, by keeping to one, single version of the Paradox, can you attain completion.

L I N E S

1. — x — The man grasps at continuity.
      Continually ominous
      if you persist in your course.
      No improvement.

In attempting to achieve consistency in your life, you have precipitously, artificially changed your course. You have become even more inconsistent. You have less continuity than before.

2. —o— He keeps to the golden mean.
      Guilt disappears.

Your ambitions are somewhat grandiose. You recognize this, along with the improbability of achieving them. Turn inward, to what it is that endures in you, the basic principles of your life. Turn inward honestly and develop the being you discover there.

3. —o— The man is disgraced
      because he does not maintain continuity.
      You will regret it
      if you keep to your course.

You are prone to embarrassing situations occurring in public. You get caught between your own character and the mood, the atmosphere of the outside world. You are hesitant, awkward; consequently you are often misguided and off the mark in your reactions to others.

4. —o— A hunting preserve without game.

You think you are trying to solve your problems; actually you are avoiding the real issue. In psychological terms, you are transferring. Face up to what is actually the source of the problem, even if it is a defect in yourself. If the source is in yourself, then it can be more easily corrected.

5. — × — The man clings to continuity.
Auspicious
for the wife.
Ominous
for the husband.

Is your life based on an allegiance, a loyalty, a fealty to someone, some idea, some organization? Then you should strongly attempt to make your character consistent. Do you exist for yourself, with all your relationships of love and loyalty based on the devotion of others to you? Then do not attempt artificially to mold yourself into a consistent, identifiable character.

6. — × — The man tries frantically to retain continuity.
Ominous.

You are in a perpetual hurry. You are always a few steps behind and a few steps in front of yourself. You are never composed, never at rest. You are always late and you never finish. Hurry up and seek out a means to find inner composure!

33

T-Hun ▪ Retreat

*The Mountain
below*

*Heaven
above*

O R A C L E

The mountain reaches from the earth
but remains beneath the sky.
The superior man keeps lesser men at a distance,
maintaining a dignified reserve.
He does not let them know what he thinks of them.

*Improvement.
Keep to your course
in minor things.*

I N T E R P R E T A T I O N

A r t h a ▪ You are opposed by active forces so powerful
that you must retreat before them. This reversal is not a capitulation. You remain as untouched by your enemies as heaven is in
falling back before a mountain peak. This retreat need not be a
desperate helter-skelter flight. It can be as proud and confident
as the retreat of the sandpiper before the incoming tide. Directions are only relative. Any reversal can be turned into an advance by reversing your goals. The improvement predicted in the
oracle can be achieved by a calm and deliberate falling back. You
cannot avoid the frustration of your present direction. Beware of
harboring hatred for those who frustrate you. Hate is a clumsy,
debilitating burden. An inspired yogi can love his enemies. The

natural man, the "superior man" of the oracles, simply disassociates himself from those who oppose him. He cannot love them. He refuses to hate them. He withdraws his emotions from the everyday world. He turns inward, toward himself and a circle of those whom he *can* love.

K a m a ▪ You and Friend are in conflict. Friend willfully blocks expressions of communication and mutual activity that you feel are essential to the relationship. To continue to try to draw Friend into the situations Friend wishes to avoid will drive Friend away. Give in to Friend's inclinations—if you value the relationship—and enjoy Friend on Friend's terms. Beware of harboring negative feelings for Friend. They can never be an element in a successful readjustment. You must learn to depend on yourself for what Friend will not give you.

M o k s h a ▪ In the practice of moksha nothing that you encounter should hinder or impede you. As your experiences change, your knowledge of the One and All changes. No matter what happens, in a manner of speaking you continue to progress. A true path to enlightenment is always flexible; never preordained; always accepting and willing—eager—to change and broaden. Your practice of moksha has become static. You refuse to accept experiences and ideas that do not fit the path you have chosen. You feel you are encountering a hostile force because your present spiritual experiences do not conform to your ideals, based on previous experiences. The opposition in this case is your own past. Your preconceptions and your rigid beliefs oppose the flow of time and events. There is only one path and you can never choose it—you can only follow it—without real progress, without real direction, without real growth—all illusions. There is only the inevitable, eternal, and constant movement of now.

L I N E S

1. — x — He turns tail.
   Peril.
   Take no action whatsoever.

You have not given yourself enough time to retreat in an orderly, rational fashion. Do not attempt any forward movement, no matter how insignificant.

2. — x — He holds to his purpose
   with an unbreakable thong
   of yellow oxhide.

In your recoil from hostile forces you have tied your fortunes to someone stronger than you who is also recoiling from them. His strength will carry you to safety.

3. — o — He is entangled
   and withdraws in danger and distress.
   Deal as generously with your oppressors
   as you would with a servant or a concubine.
   Auspicious.

Your falling back from a hostile force has been halted by the unlooked-for interference of a third force. You are frustrated and in danger. If you can somehow establish a community of interest with the newcomer he may, instead of hindering you, facilitate your withdrawal.

4. — o — He withdraws
   although he would rather not.
   Auspicious for the great;
   unattainable by the small.

Fall back bravely and naturally, without hatred, without regrets, and without loss of self-esteem. Accept events as emanations of God, not as reflections on yourself. If you rankle with hatred, cringe with regrets and hate yourself, even a well-planned, well-accomplished withdrawal will harm you psychologically.

5. ——o—— He withdraws sensibly.
   Auspicious
   if you keep to your course.

All those threatened by the same hostile force recognize their common purpose and bond. With very little discussion everyone has agreed to work together for a successful withdrawal. As long as this spirit continues, all goes well.

6. ——o—— He withdraws nobly.
   Improvement
   in every way.

This is the falling back of the enlightened man who knows neither forward nor backward. It is the reversal of the whistling hobo. He approaches a river; the bridge is down; he cannot cross. He returns the way he came. Not once did his whistled song miss a beat or lose its proper pitch.

34

Teh-Khwang ▪ Great Strength

*Heaven
below*

*Thunder
above*

O R A C L E

Thunder rages above heaven.
The superior man is especially proper,
whatever he does.

*Improvement
if you keep to your course.*

I N T E R P R E T A T I O N

A r t h a ▪ This is a time of great influence for you. Your
Tao is strong. It has an external function as well as an internal
force. Your direction is appreciated and followed by others. Caution: do not abuse this influence. One abuse would be consciously
to take advantage of those under your influence. This would be
clearly and unequivocally corrupt. But you can also abuse your
influence by failing to recognize it. Do not, through false modesty
or neurotic self-deprecation or for any other reason, ignore your
own power. This not only denies your own Tao, but is also unfair
to those whom you influence. Your proper position is in the
center. Everyone in your circle relates to you. If your movement
is outgoing, strong, unfettered, then you will give strength to
those around you and they in turn will support you. But if your
movement is inward, weak, inhibited, you will only succeed in
drawing others down into the chaos of your personal life, causing

disillusionment, anxieties, and conflicts. This is a strong, creative hexagram and bodes well as long as the responsibilities implied in it aren't shirked.

K a m a ▪ Friend is extremely susceptible to you. If you are glum, then Friend will soon be glum; if you are feeling silly, then Friend will soon be feeling silly; if you express an interest in a certain idea, then Friend will soon be interested in the same thing; and if you devote yourself to loving Friend, then Friend will soon be devoted to loving you. The paradox of power is evident in this situation. Friend, who is entirely under your influence, nevertheless can react freely and spontaneously to you. You, who are under no influence, must react carefully and thoughtfully because of the responsibilities placed on you by your influence on Friend. Like other paradoxes, this is the expression of the inevitable balance of the forces of Yin and Yang.

M o k s h a ▪ Your path to enlightenment lies in your ability to bring enlightenment to others. Enlightenment is the passage from an intellectual belief in an abstract, conceptual "universal" truth, to existentially *being* that truth; passage from an idea to an all-embracing, universal being. You, particularly, make this passage when you extend your intellectual, conceptual understanding to others. As your mind meets with others in common understanding, the universality of what you believe strikes you in a way beyond mind and beyond intellect and the experience of teaching becomes a religious one. Denial of this by you would be hypocritical and spiritually defeating.

L I N E S

1. ——o—— The man gathers his strength in his toes.
    Definitely ominous
    if you advance.

You feel frustrated. But do not be rash.

2. —o— *Auspicious*
   if you keep to your course.

You are at the beginning of something. You feel exuberant and optimistic. If you get too carried away, you will not be able to react effectively to counter any obstacles that arise, or to adjust to any changes that occur. Maintain an inner equilibrium.

3. —o— The small man uses up all his strength.
   The superior man conserves it.
   The ram butts against a fence,
   entangling his horns.
   Danger
   if you keep to your course.

You have been so successful in the past that you believe that the proper reaction to obstacles is simply to ignore them and to press forward. Danger: overconfidence. Remain always open to the possibility that you may have to slow down, compromise, or even retreat in order to follow your Tao.

4. —o— The ram butts against the fence.
   He breaks through, untangled.
   A large wagon
   depends on the strength of each wheel spoke.
   Auspicious
   if you keep to your course.
   Guilt disappears.

Because you can avoid the abuse of influence, mentioned in the "Artha" section above, your influence is a constructive, creative force in your environment.

5. —x— His easy life destroys his ramlike qualities.
   Without guilt.

Previous circumstances in your life have made you instinctively belligerent and stubborn. But the circumstances now have changed. Change your behavior as well. The world is much more friendly toward you now. You have influence in it. Open up. Be sympathetic and tolerant.

6. — x — The ram is stuck in the fence.
         He can neither retreat nor advance.
         No improvement in any way.
         Auspicious
         if you accept your position.

You are in a seemingly inescapable bind. Any move you make
forward, backward, or sideways will bring contention, conflict,
and more complicated entanglements. Your only way out is to
relinquish all ambitions, abandon all goals, and free yourself of
the illusion of hope.

35

Tzhin ▪ Advance

The Earth
below

The Sun
above

O R A C L E

The sun shines above the earth.
The superior man polishes his brilliance.
He secures civil tranquillity
and is rewarded with many horses.
He is interviewed three times a day.

Improvement.

I N T E R P R E T A T I O N

A r t h a ▪ This hexagram represents the sun rising over
the earth. The sun gives light while it destroys itself; the dark,
receptive earth turns the sun's energy into life and growth. Two
people are involved in this hexagram: one is passionate, energetic, prophetic, and self-destructive; the other is impression-
able, passive, logical, and blooming. Most likely you are the
latter, passive half of the pair. The passionate partner is usually
not the type of person who consults the I Ching oracle. Search
out the one who is your alter ego, your negative self, your opposite pole, the Yang to your Yin. Acknowledge that the force
behind what you do comes from him. Working together, you will
make important advances and new discoveries. Keep in mind the
relationship between the earth and the sun: set aside all petty

considerations, superficial judgments based on selfish values. Love without reservation the sun that turns your darkness to light. If you do happen to be the passionate half of this pair—the radiant sun—nothing said in this oracle can make any impression on you: your demon is too strong. The advancement of this hexagram will not come from either half of the pair alone; it is the result of the interaction between them.

K a m a ▪ You and Friend are well matched. Your characters neatly complement each other (see "Artha" section). Together you have the potential for a creative, evolving, and extended relationship. The only problems you may encounter result from your clinging to the stale concepts of a destructive tradition. The passionate partner (the sun) and the passive partner (the earth) need not be man and woman respectively. If the passionate one, the Yang force in the relationship, is the woman and the passive, Yin partner is the man, then the man is likely to feel that his role is "not normal." False pride will cause anxiety and conflict. He must forget the generally accepted concepts of roles and accept and appreciate his own character. He must base the relationship on that—not on his ideas (actually, his culture's ideas) of what the relationship should be. If the passionate one is the man and the passive one is the woman, then the danger is that the woman may impose her political principles on the relationship. Although she feels a natural resentment at society's discrimination against women generally, she must also accept and appreciate her own personal "feminine" traits of passivity and receptiveness, which are part of her own character and not solely due to her gender.

M o k s h a ▪ You must search for the one who will enlighten you. He is not a guru, not a priest, not a teacher, not a savant. He does not intend to enlighten you and, in fact, does not intend anything. He burns brightly, with passion and without purpose. He is as lost without you as you are without him. His light dies if you do not reflect it. Your life is dark without his light.

L I N E S

1. — x — The man wishes to advance
and is held back.
Auspicious
if you keep to your course.
If you cannot inspire trust
accept it graciously.

You hesitate to make contact with the one whose creative energy
and power will improve both your fortunes. You fear a rebuff.
Because of the other's passionate and choleric nature, a rebuff by
him is certainly a possibility. But do not let that restrain you in
your efforts to reach him. If you are rebuffed, remain calm.

2. — x — The man advances,
yet is full of sorrow.
Auspicious
if you keep to your course,
by the grace of your grandmother.

You cannot reach the one on whose creative energy and power your
mutual fortune depends. The very energy and power of his that
you are seeking are the obstacles that keep you from reaching him.
Your life is one of womanly grief and despair. The feminine energy, the Yin force, that radiates from your grief and despair will
take the place of the masculine power, the Yang force, that you
cannot attain. With the enfolding and comforting strength of your
own grief, you will find happiness and fulfillment in your life, although on a different plane from what you now envision.

3. — x — He is trusted by all.
No guilt.

Although you are personally weak and ineffectual, you have the
state of mind and the intelligence to be able to participate in the
activities of others, sharing mutual trust and understanding.
Yin and Yang are evenly balanced in you.

4. —o— He advances like a groundhog.
Peril
if you keep to your course.

You are accustomed to moving stealthily, inconspicuously—like a rodent that moves at night. Secrecy is important to your advancement. But you are entering the sphere of someone whose perceptivity and brilliance will discover you and expose your movements. Beware.

5. — x — *Guilt disappears.*
Do not let success concern you.
Auspicious
if you advance.
Improvement
no matter what you do.

You live in complete accord with the creative forces in your life. You advance through the combination of your receptive personality with someone else's passionate personality. Your progress depends on *both of you* for its continuing existence, and for its direction. Since the direction of your progress is dependent on another as well as yourself, it may not be exactly what you envisioned. But it *is* the best way, the right way, and the only way for you. Any regrets you have are based only on illusions. They will soon disappear.

6. — o — He advances
horns first.
He uses them to punish rebels
within his own city.
Peril.
Auspicious.
Keep to your course
despite any regrets.

Although you are generally a passive person, you must now take positive action. The obstacles you face are the result of your own misguided activity. Only an active and energetic destruction of these obstacles will enable you to proceed. And only *you* can do it. Be careful not to extend your aggressive energies beyond what is required. Do not try to influence situations other than this particular one.

36

Ming-Ee ▪ Darkening of the Light

*The Sun
below*

*The Earth
above*

O R A C L E

The sun sets behind the earth.
The superior man manages others.
He proves he is intelligent
by keeping quiet about it.

*Keep to your course.
Be aware of the difficulties ahead.*

I N T E R P R E T A T I O N

A r t h a ▪ You are in the intolerable position of being
under the authority of forces that are contrary to your principles and beliefs. Instead of just being irrelevant, on a different
plane, the underlying direction of the outside forces that direct,
shape, and limit the circumstances of your life confront your
own philosophy and ideology head-on. There is nothing you can
do to change this situation. You must, in fact, accept the continuing existence of this darkness that envelops your life. You
will always see it as darkness opposed to your light, as a lie
opposed to your truth, as evil opposed to your good. But
because the scope of this dark authority is so wide and because

its influence is so pervasive, you will be forced to accede to its impetus on all levels of your life except the most personal. You are alone among your acquaintances in your condemnation of these dark forces. Other people either condone them or maintain a laissez-faire attitude. No one would be receptive to any initiatives to change or destroy the powers that be, at least at present. You must resign yourself, in fact, to being a slave—for the time being. You must not rock the boat. You must hide your real feelings. You must be blind to the evil surrounding you. This is a shameful time for you. But while being forced into all these sins of omission, you must never allow yourself to fall into a sin of commission. Don't give in to your oppressors to the extent of acting on their behalf. When it comes to your *reactions*, you must submit; but your *actions* must always be pure and correct, according to your own principles, no matter what the cost.

K a m a ▪ Your relationship with Friend seems grotesque and unhappy. It is the opposite of everything you want it to be. You don't know whether Friend is the originator of this travesty or whether you both are guilty. While the impulses and emotions that bind you together seem to *you* to be directly contrary to your principles and declarations of love, Friend sees nothing wrong at all. Any attempt to communicate the violence of your anxiety and the depth of your despair only offends Friend and leads to more unhappiness. As for a possible origin of these negative feelings: consider the fact that the reality (as you see it) is directly contrary to *your* ideals only, not to Friend's. Friend doesn't see a problem at all. Friend accepts the relationship as it is. You have a self-defeating impulse to look for whatever is not there, instead of finding what *is* there. You form your ideals not from what the relationship is, but from what it *isn't*. Successful psychoanalysis would bring to light the sources of your contrariness and assist in destroying them. Religious enlightenment would eradicate the ideals and expectations that are the cause of *all* suffering in man.

M o k s h a ▪ With enlightenment, (1) absolute freedom is realized and (2) the ego disappears. In his absolute freedom the enlightened one acts in perfect harmony with the universal flux. The deepest, darkest evil—the sin of Lucifer—is to experience the first and reject the second: to realize ultimate freedom without humility. This is the hexagram of the black magician, the exploiter of wisdom.

L I N E S

1. —o— The man flies,
    but his wings droop.
    If the superior man continually leaves home
    he may go three days without eating.
    Wherever he goes, people scorn him.

Blithely believing you could avoid your problems simply by ignoring them has led you into a disastrous situation. You have clashed with the efforts and ambitions of everyone else. If you insist on sticking to your principles you will be reviled and opposed, even by those closest to you. If you compromise, you will lose your own self-respect. Withdraw from everything.

2. —x— The man is wounded in the left thigh.
    He saves himself on a swift horse.
    Auspicious.

The encroachment of darkness is not yet irreversible. You can still salvage the situation. There are others besides yourself who recognize the danger. Join with them.

3. —o— Hunting on friendly ground at night,
    he shoots the lord of the dark regions.
    *Do not try to rectify everything
    all at once.*

Considering the dark and dangerous period you are in, you have taken a somewhat cavalier and diffident attitude toward men and events. You refuse to recognize that the prevailing darkness is relevant to you and go right on your merry way—straight into trouble. You have accidentally injured someone who plays an important role in the social system you have so blithely ignored. This is more grave than just stepping on someone's toes. You have caused real injury and you must expect real retribution.

4. — x — He enters the belly of the dark regions
          through the left side;
          his brightness is dimmed
          and he slips quietly out at the gate.

You have been thrust into the midst of a repressive and tyrannical situation. But you have nothing to fear. You figure so little in the oppressor's plans that you will be ignored completely.

5. — x — The dark times of Prince Chi.
          Keep to your course.

Prince Chi played the same role in an evil court as did Hamlet. Feigning insanity, his obvious antagonism toward the king was overlooked. But while Hamlet at last became a man of action, dealing vengeance and retribution, Prince Chi remained inactive and contented himself with successfully avoiding having to compromise his principles.

6. — x — Neither dark nor light,
          only obscurity.
          He ascends above the roof of heaven;
          he will descend below the crust of the earth.

The adverse forces that rule your life have extended themselves so far, have fulfilled themselves so terribly completely, that little by little they have become meaningless. As they have accomplished their dark metamorphosis, their purposes stand revealed as meaningless and illusory, like the serpent who eats himself. Your patient suffering has also fulfilled itself and will soon be finally relieved by the natural, inevitable flux from Yin to Yang, from negative to affirmative, from dark to light.

37

Khyeh-Zhain · The Family

The Sun
below

The Wind
above

ORACLE

Wind passes above the fire
and warms the family.
The superior man is careful to be always truthful
and consistent in his conduct.
The wife keeps to her course.

Keep to your course.

INTERPRETATION

Artha · In terms of the extremely patriarchal mores of ancient China are you the "husband" figure or the "wife" in the situation for which you have consulted the oracle? Do you control the circumstances? or are you controlled? Do you have authority? or are you under authority? Are you teaching? or are you learning? Do your own principles shape the situation? or do another's principles apply? If you are a "husband" then your problems stem from hypocrisy on your part: you say one thing and do another. You yourself do not act according to the principles you apply to others. You don't practice what you preach. You must either adjust your actions to fit your expressed principles or you must change your expressed principles. A dissimilarity between your demands on others and your demands on yourself confuses those who depend on you for direction. If you are a "wife," your problem is that for some reason—most likely a very good reason—you are rebelling against the authority in this particular situation. You have forgotten that the relationship between yourself and the authority is not based on power, but on a common bond. E.g., between a husband and wife, the bond is love; between business partners there is a common goal of a fair profit; among members of a service organization there is the common purpose of charitable works. Instead of rebelling destructively against an unfortunately weak or dishonest authority, you should recognize the authority's defects and adjust your notions to it so as not to weaken the other, more important bond: the original raison d'être of the relationship.

K a m a ▪ There is an ambiguity about who is responsible for making decisions affecting you and Friend as a couple. You and Friend are not in such a state of entwined bliss that your thoughts and desires always coincide. And yet you are not independent enough—either practically or psychologically—to go your own ways. You must confer and agree together which of you is responsible for making which decision in which areas of mutual activity. And when a decision is made by one, the other should not judge it—should not be resentful or deprecatory or analytical or even grateful. You must each maintain a complete and calm acceptance of the will of the other in matters for which—by mutual consent—one of you has been made responsible.

M o k s h a ▪ The Oneness of all things has been revealed to you. Everything is Buddha—yourself also. You *know* it completely, but you don't live it. When you see a flower, you pick only a flower. When you see a fly, you kill only a fly. When you meet someone else, you treat him only as if he were someone else. On your path to enlightenment you must cease making distinctions. The differences between flower, fly, someone else, and yourself are only illusions.

L I N E S

1. —o— The man makes rules for the family.
   Guilt disappears.

You have just begun an activity in which you hold expressed
authority and heavy responsibilities. If, from the very beginning, your authority is weak and indecisive, those involved with
you will always be faltering and confused. If you do not accept
your responsibilities from the very outset, the relationship between you and your associates will always be one of mutual
mistrust and secretiveness.

2. —x— She attends to the cooking.
   Auspicious
   if you keep to your course.

Enough responsibility has already been placed on your shoul-
ders. You should not seek any more responsibilities, but concentrate on fulfilling those you have now.

3. —o— The man is very stern.
   If he let his wife and children chatter and giggle
   he would regret it.
   Auspicious,
   but with guilt
   and peril.

In some areas of your life there is a wide range of activity open to
you. In other areas you are bound by strict limitations. It is easier
and seems more fulfilling to restrict your activities to the sphere
in which you have greater freedom. But you do have responsibilities in the more limited sphere, where action is more difficult
and seems less rewarding. If you concentrate only on your
broader powers you will succumb to selfish, egotistical tempta-
tions. If you cannot find a balance between the two it is better to
concentrate on your sphere of limited activity and let the other go
for a while. That way you can at least avoid betraying your own
deepest principles.

4. — x — She enriches the family.
   Very auspicious.

You have the happy ability to deal harmoniously with the material world. You are skillful and clever, fair and unselfish. You bring good things to yourself and to those close to you.

5. —o— He is a king to his own household.
   No anxiety.
   Auspicious.

You are so sure of yourself that others respect and follow you. You are so free of anxieties that you treat everyone with love.

6. —o— The man is sincere and clothed in glory.
   Auspicious
   in the end.

If your responsibilities and your relationships have increased, your character must also alter. You must take into account the new responsibility implied by your new and as yet untried influence on others.

38

Khway · Neutrality

 The Marsh
below

 The Sun
above

O R A C L E

Fire over the marsh.
The superior man allows
variations within the norm.

Success
in minor matters.

I N T E R P R E T A T I O N

A r t h a ▪ Man is a mix and a flux of two opposing forces.
Yin and Yang, active and passive, optimistic and pessimistic,
extroverted and introverted, beautiful and ugly are a few of the
different visions of this dualism. An individual's character and
psyche are based on a unique interaction of these contrasting
forces. This hexagram represents a stand-off neutrality between
the counteracting forces within you. Fire naturally rises; water
naturally settles. In their position in this hexagram (trigram *Li*,
Fire, is above trigram *Tui*, the Marsh) there is no interaction
between them. The traditional interpretation of this hexagram is
that you are involved in a situation where two opposing view-
points, two opposing sides, irreconcilably neutralize themselves
into a stalemate. But since *you* are the subject of the hexagram,
it is clear that the polarization indicated is not an incidental,
outside phenomenon, but is basic to *your* course, the essence of
your Tao: it is within you. You constantly feel pulled in opposite
directions. Whenever you consider acting, inactivity seems just

as desirable. Whatever you want you also think you'd just as well not have. Whatever you believe, its opposite seems to have just as much validity. Whatever you say, you regret. You are not in a state of neurotic indecisiveness, although it might seem so. You bear a relativistic view of things, a kind of metaphysical fairness. In small, unimportant matters this is a strong position because of its basic balance, calm and good judgment. In larger, more far-reaching undertakings, however, you lack the unfettered force that would give your activity a constant, definite direction, and you lack the spiritual depth to accept the patterns of opposites within you and flow spontaneously with them. In your dealings with other people your evenness and lack of predisposition recommend you for small tasks. In broader activities that involve deeply held principles and ideals, your lack of a definite position makes you seem unpredictable and untrustworthy—not implying dishonesty or impetuousness, but in terms of the ambitions of others. Because of your basic neutrality, however, you may be called on to judge between factions in a dispute.

K a m a ▪ Because of your inner polarity (see "Artha" section) you are unable to enter fully into your relationship with Friend. From Friend's point of view, the relationship is always unfulfilled, weighty, mired. It may seem to Friend that you are holding back, that you are reticent in your feelings and afraid to express your emotions. On whatever levels your relationship *does* function, it is free of conflict, free of turbulence, and, at least on your part, free of egoism, selfishness, and possessiveness.

M o k s h a ▪ Your spiritual life is based on the revelation of dualism. You should study the abstract polarities within the spiritual system you follow. For a Christian it is the meaning of God and the devil; for a Taoist it is the opposition of Yin and Yang; for an existentialist it is the distinction between man's essential nature and the phenomenal universe; for a Buddhist it is the state of desire as opposed to nirvana. This is a wise and thoughtful vision. When these basic opposites are reconciled and experienced as one, perfect enlightenment is possible.

L I N E S

1. —o— He has lost his horses.
       He need not search for them;
       they will return by themselves.
       If he meets bad men
       he can speak with them.
       Guilt disappears.

Your polarized state is new. You feel that you have lost something. You have. Because of your new inner neutralization, your values, your direction, and your principles, offset by the force of their opposites, have lost their traditional meaning for you. But remember, this has all happened *within you;* it is your Tao, your direction now. Do not regret these things. Do not anxiously grasp at old ideals. You are likely to come into contact with unprincipled and willful people. You cannot avoid them, nor can you—since you are neutral—hope to influence or oppose them. You can be careful and guard against thoughtless mistakes.

2. —o— He meets his master in an alley.
       No mistakes.

Your ambiguity about a factional dispute makes your relationship with a close friend, who is involved in the dispute, embarrassing from his point of view. It pains him, but he feels he must avoid you. Sympathize, without pride or anger. Arrange an "accidental" meeting in a secluded place. It will be welcome, pleasant, and fruitful for both of you.

3. —x— They pull back his carriage
       and drive back his team of oxen.
       His head is shaved;
       his nose is cut off.
       A bad beginning;
       a good ending.

Everything goes wrong. Whatever you do is blocked and reversed. Whatever you say is misunderstood. You are conspired against, reviled, and denigrated. Just keep a grip on yourself. It

will not last forever. The good fortune which will follow will be
equal in degree to your present misfortune.

4. —o— The man stands alone amid conflict.
He meets good men
and together they find common cause and
sympathy.
Peril,
but no mistakes.

You have met someone who is like you in his inner neutrality. The
same problems cloud his life as yours. If the relationship is kept at
a low key, you can both overcome your basic isolation.

5. —x— He clings with his teeth
to his friend and relation.
Can you make a mistake
advancing with such aid?

Your noncommittal, relativistic balance of judgment generally
keeps you from getting involved in the activity of others. But you
are becoming emotionally involved with someone else who, with
love and companionship, has cut through your isolation to your
heart. If you are moved, then join the other, even if the only
principle for your doing so is an emotional attachment.

6. —o— The man stands alone amid conflict.
Something approaches;
a pig covered with mud;
a carriage full of ghosts.
He draws his bow and then relaxes it;
it is not an assailant,
but a close relative.
Advance
into the gentle rain.
Auspicious.

You mistake the motives of someone who approaches you in friendship. You believe that it is a coldhearted, selfish effort to win you
over. You put up all your defenses and ignore the other person,
avoid and degrade him. But the other is sincere in his friendship.
You must eventually open yourself up and accept this sincerity.

39

Khyen · Difficulty

The Mountain
below

The Deep
above

O R A C L E

The lake in the volcano.
The superior man looks inward
and cultivates his virtue.

Remain on friendly ground
and avoid hostile territory.
Confer with the great man.
Auspicious
if you keep to your course.

I N T E R P R E T A T I O N

A r t h a ▪ You have met with difficulties. These difficulties are inherent and unavoidable in the path you have chosen,
in your Tao. They are not a sudden, catastrophic, hostile phenomenon. If anyone is responsible for these difficulties it is yourself:
meeting with difficulties is an inevitable, essential hazard in the
course you have chosen for yourself. These are not obstacles in
their own natures. Your reaction to them makes them obstacles.
Things are difficult only because you consider them to be difficult. There is nothing wrong in being aware of your course and
persisting in it; but it *is* an error to set distant goals and to
establish an ideal pattern for the future. This is the error that

makes your present situation seem difficult. You need someone to advise you, someone who can teach you—not how to abolish the obstacles or circumvent them or overcome them, but how to accept them with peace of mind.

K a m a ▪ A conflict has suddenly arisen between you and Friend over something specific, something heretofore outside your relationship. This could be a third person to whom you each react differently, or an event which you view differently, or some other newly appeared aspect of your relationship which is causing tension and contention. Obviously some conflict was bound to appear sooner or later, about one thing or another. Instead of trying to overcome this specific difficulty by compromise or by one of you assuming authority in the matter (such slapdash solutions can cause spitefulness on one part and regrets on the other), ignore the difficulty for a while; withdraw from it. Return to your convivial state before the difficulty appeared. Of course you both will remain conscious of the difficulty. But the love and pleasure and time you share will encompass and overcome the latent difficulty which you also share. When it arises naturally again out of your lives together, you can meet it together and react spontaneously, as a couple.

M o k s h a ▪ The fact that you have met with difficulties in your spiritual path indicates that it is a path encumbered by such unspiritual karma as goals, desires, ideologies, and theories. Free your spiritual path of such maya and you will achieve enlightenment; free your whole life of them and you will achieve Brahma.

L I N E S

1. — x — Either the man advances
and encounters great difficulties
or he stands still
and earns praise.

Advancing is Yang; standing still is Yin. You can either advance, move out and leave behind those you love; or you can stand still, remaining where you are among those you love.

2. — x — The man encounters one difficulty after another.
        Still, he conscientiously pursues his mission.

If *you* alone were the only one involved in your difficulties, retreat and withdrawal would be the best course. But you have a responsibility to someone else to meet the difficulties head-on. You are definitely committed to it.

3. — o — Either the man advances
        and encounters great difficulties
        or stands still
        with his former allies.

In this case your responsibility to others is the reason you must *not* meet the difficulties head-on. There are others who depend on you and who would suffer with you in your attempt to overcome the difficulties that have appeared.

4. — x — Either the man advances
        and encounters great difficulties
        or stands still,
        forming alliances.

You need the support of others to overcome the difficulties that beset you. If you believe that your friends automatically will support you, you are mistaken. Hold back awhile. Talk it over with your friends and colleagues. Tell them the details and discuss the ramifications of the situation. They will support you when they feel involved enough and informed enough to do so.

5. — x — The man struggles with the greatest difficulties;
        his friends come to the rescue.

The problem you are facing is essentially not your problem. It is a difficulty in the life of someone you know and you have taken it on as an act of love because of a sense of responsibility to the other. Because you are not directly involved and because of the generous spirit that has induced you to take this problem on, any

efforts you make to overcome it will be successful. You should go
as far as you are able; others will join you on your friend's behalf
and things will be solved quickly and satisfactorily.

6. — x — Either the man advances
           and encounters great difficulties
           or stands still,
           finding fulfillment.
           Auspicious
           if you confer with the great man.

The difficulty in this case is not an element in your own life alone;
the difficulty is more general—a social, cultural one. It throws a
pall over your quiet and undisturbed life. You would like to ignore
it, disregard it. Ironically, the objective, uninvolved course you
have chosen has enabled you better to perceive general wrongs
and evils. And this perception affects you emotionally and draws
you back into the world of subjectivity and involvement. In this
line "advancing" refers to continuing on your path of complete
acceptance—retreat from the world of values and difficulties.
"Standing still" refers to remaining within the world of values
and difficulties. The auspiciousness of the oracle depends on the
result of the enlightened, objective, and unselfish attitude with
which you face your difficulties. Do not ignore the outside world.
If you do, you will meet with other, inward difficulties, the
results of regret and feelings of guilt that will be much harder to
bear and even more tenacious than the present outward difficulties.

40

Khieh · Release

The Deep
below

Thunder
above

O R A C L E

The thunder rolls,
releasing a cloudburst.
The superior man stays on friendly ground.
He forgives errors
and deals gently with those who wrong him.

Auspicious
to act soon
if action is called for.
Auspicious
to return to your proper course
if no action is called for.

I N T E R P R E T A T I O N

A r t h a · This is the hexagram of climax, of the dramatic
finale, of the miraculous release. The situation you are in is
similar to the hero's in the *Symphonie Fantastique* or the *Beggar's Opera:* the messenger with the king's reprieve gallops
madly toward the gallows. You are saved! Or are about to be. If
you are still in danger, do not, because of this favorable oracle,
relax your guard. Your rescue is *almost* inevitable, but you must
not change your present last-ditch stance. If you *are* safe and
sound at last, do not dwell on the past—its dangers and your

fears, its deliverance and your exultation. Return to the simple, uneventful life you led before the danger developed. Reassume the same proper and fitting role you played in the past. However, do not try to resume any projects which were interrupted when you were plunged into danger. Note the condemned soldier's tale in *The Idiot*. On his ride to the gallows, instead of concentrating on his (seemingly hopeless) danger and his chances for salvation, the condemned man lets himself go, gives up his ego, and slips into the brilliant vision of a religious experience. He becomes acutely aware of his surroundings, as if he is seeing the world for the first time, entering a new existential reality for the (supposedly) final five minutes of his life. He is saved from the gallows by a last-minute reprieve. In an effort to recapture that momentary vision of his trip to the gallows he turns to drink and dies of acute alcoholism five years later. Unlike the condemned soldier, you are aware of your coming release. The danger is that you may lose yourself in the extreme joy of your supposed salvation as he lost himself in his extreme despair. You must remain cool and aware at this time in order to avoid a psychological slump, a spiritual chasm after you are out of danger.

K a m a ▪ The climax of this hexagram is not a zenith, like a sexual climax, but a nadir, a low point in your relationship with Friend. You and Friend are at the end of a trying and almost disastrous time of conflicts and selfish pressures. The embrace of reconciliation, which is imminent, if not already accomplished, is the response of sincere lovers to their rising passions in times of anger and stress. It is a response full of hope. Do not fall back into the stubborn positions that sparked your conflict, but wipe the slate clean—assume you both were wrong then and that you both will be right now.

M o k s h a ▪ Enlightenment comes to some after a close brush with death. Enlightenment *is* death of a sort. The Zen Buddhist experiencing satori "dies" as he loses his identity; the yogi abolishes his ego and thus "dies"; the LSD tripper experiences an involuntary, chemically induced illusory death. In one way or another you were so close to death that in your mind you already died and you experienced existence free of all illusions, including that of your own selfhood. This experience has provided you with a strong enough revelation to form your life's spiritual path. Remain humble in the face of this experience. If you begin to regard it egotistically, you may begin to think of it as having been a resurrection, with all the grandeur that implies: danger!

L I N E S

1. — x — *No mistakes.*

   Feel no guilt at being singled out by fortune.

2. — o — The man bags three foxes
   and obtains the golden arrows.
   Auspicious
   if you keep to your course.

Your release has come about because someone for whom you performed a service has used his power to place you in a position of responsibility away from the danger that now threatens you. The service you performed in the first place was impulsive and spontaneously selfless. Now you must fulfill your new responsibilities with forethought and careful consideration.

3. — x — The porter transports his burden
   in a carriage.
   This will only tempt robbers.
   If you keep to your course
   you will regret it.

Although you have been released from danger you are not able to slough off the anxieties and humiliations of those last moments of imminent disaster. This makes you extremely vulnerable to those who are envious of your good fortune. A victor who feels defeated is easy game for the greedy.

4. — o — Let your toes go;
   friends come,
   mutual confidence arises.

In your time of need, the time of danger, you depended somewhat on a person not entirely trustworthy or sympathetic to you. Your release from danger must also be a release from this person. As soon as you relinquish his aid someone else more suitable and reliable will be able to help you.

5. — x — The man releases himself
        and earns the confidence
        of those who held him.
        Auspicious.

Release will come only if you move deeply, genuinely in the Tao of this hexagram. This moving line indicates that, contrary to the general meaning of this hexagram, your release is not at all assured and you yourself are the only means of your own release. If you can save yourself, the sincerity and presence of mind that was required on your part will be appreciated and honored by others. If it comes, release will bring you good fortune beyond just your escape from danger.

6. — x — The man shoots at a falcon high on the wall
        and hits it.
        Improvement
        in every way.

This line indicates a symbolic salvation from symbolic or abstract dangers. Catching sight of the moon on a stormy night would be such a symbolic release. The spiritual effect of this experience will infuse your life with new meaning and depth.

41

Sun ▪ Decrease

*The Marsh
below*

*The Mountain
above*

O R A C L E

A marsh at the foot of the mountain.
The man restrains his anger
and represses his desires.

Very auspicious.
No mistakes.
You may take any action you wish.
Keep to your course.
What is your course?
Sacrifice two baskets of grain,
even if that is all you have.

I N T E R P R E T A T I O N

A r t h a ▪ This hexagram indicates the time of a decrease of some sort in your life. It could simply mean a loss of material possessions. It could also mean a diminishing of activity, of pleasure, or of social contacts. Whichever or whatever recently has played a large role in your life will now diminish. There is certainly nothing to worry about. For every gain—and you have just experienced a time of gain—there is a corresponding loss. This is not bad unless you cling to the great value you have learned to place on gain. Now is the time to return to more basic values. Value the simplicity of your new way of life in this time of loss.

K a m a ▪ Like everything else, love relationships go through cycles of increase and decrease. For friends and lovers, such times of decrease are often times of anxiety and despondency. They try to retain the heights of love. They regret the decrease of passion in themselves and in each other. You and Friend are in such a time. You have reached your peak and now are on your way down, into the more mundane world. Other things besides *you* will regain Friend's interest. Don't become jealous or spiteful about them. Other things besides *Friend* will regain *your* interest. Don't regret this replacement. Enter fully into what you are doing. If you see signs that Friend is anxious, reassure Friend of your love. Your relationship will decrease to a simpler, more everyday state. Attune yourself to the beauties and joys of being ordinary together.

M o k s h a ▪ Even one who has been united with the One and All—the saint, the bodhisattva—must "decrease" and reenter the wheel of karma. After a time of revelations and spiritual landmarks you will now become a little more ordinary. You will find your mind wandering to mundane matters. If you truly have been enlightened you will accept and love your role in the material world. Instead of seeking union with God through your psyche, you now can be at One through simply *being*. In this time of decrease you will become one of the simpler things, which you know are in notoriously close touch with the One and All. Any anxieties about the decrease of your spiritual involvement will lead to the deepest despair.

L I N E S

1. —o— The man suspends his activity
        and rushes to the aid of another.
        No mistakes,
        but consider carefully
        how far you can go.

Once very active, you have been forced to give up your work for a time. You can use your stymied energies to help others in what they are doing. But bear in mind that your motive must be truly altruistic and not just a need to use up your pent-up energies. It could be that your inclusion in their affairs could be an imposition on others, and even a hindrance to their accomplishing what they wish, in their own way.

2. —o— He can bring gain to another
         without incurring loss on his own part.
         Keep to your course.
         Ominous
         if you take any action.

You are pressed to do something against your principles. If you give in: misfortune. Your first responsibility to others is to consistently be yourself.

3. —x— Three men walk together:
         one man drops out.
         Walking alone, he finds a friend.

You are in an impossible triangle. One person must go. It could be you. If so, you will quickly find someone else's company.

4. —x— The man diminishes his problem
         by summoning the aid
         of someone who is glad to help.
         No mistakes.

Fortunately, there is someone who is eager to help you. The aid you require from him gives him a chance to fulfill himself. And you are not placed under heavy obligations which, in other cases of aid rendered, can cause tension between friends.

5. —x— He is presented with ten pairs
         of tortoiseshells for divination,
         and is not allowed to refuse them.
         Very auspicious.

This is a period of natural good luck for you. Good things will just fall into your lap.

6. ——o—— He brings gain to others
without incurring loss on his own part.
He will find men to help him,
many from every clan.
No mistakes.
Auspicious
if you keep to your course.
You may take any action you wish.

You will be very successful as long as your success does not
depend on exploiting the lives of others in any way. Do not worry
about finding help—your ethical attitude assures you of loyal
friends wherever you go and whatever you do.

42

Yee ▪ Increase

*Thunder
below*

*The Wind
above*

O R A C L E

The wind and thunder reinforce each other.
The superior man reinforces his good traits,
but not his bad ones.

*Improvement
in every activity.
You may cross the great water.*

I N T E R P R E T A T I O N

A r t h a ▪ There are some people who are genuinely willing to make real sacrifices for others. Often generosity is not selfless; generous acts are expected to bring a certain return, recompense in some form: a tax deduction, status, devotion, ego gratification, the assuaging of guilt are examples. In some cases charitable acts become exchanges, trades, barters. But this is truly a time of increase for *you* because *others* are willing to make real selfless sacrifices for the common good; to give and not to receive; to let go something of themselves without exacting something to replace it. This is a favorable time for you, a good time to carry out a major undertaking or to make a great change in your life. Surrounded by such goodness you should be able to detect faults in yourself and begin to rid yourself of them.

K a m a ▪ In love, as in everything else, the generous act is often not as generous as it appears. But Friend is truly generous toward you. Friend makes no unconscious claims on you. Friend's generous acts, Friend's affection and support, are all given without expectation of getting something in return. It may seem to you that *you* are the more generous of the two. Perhaps you even feel some sort of resentment about it. But: if you are resentful, then you are disappointed; if you are disappointed, it indicates that you maintain expectations; if you maintain expectations, your so-called generosity is nothing more than goods offered in trade. Friend refuses to make the trade—Friend does not see loving as merchandising. You feel hurt. If you can suspend your demands for long enough to get a clear view of Friend and Friend's actions and their motivation, you will, by contrast, discover how ungenerous your own neurotic claims are. Then you can begin to get rid of them.

M o k s h a ▪ Your spiritual path is one of self-sacrifice. It may be a path of good works, a path of self-inflicted pain, or a path of unrecompensed teaching. In any case your spiritual fulfillment depends upon your own sacrifices for the enrichment of others. Enlightenment in any form is the loss of the ego. Your path is the conscious, direct, willful giving of your ego to the One and All.

L I N E S

1. ——o—— Reinforced, he makes great changes.
   Very auspicious.
   No guilt.

With good feeling and generosity abounding this is the time to accomplish your most important designs. Whatever great effort you most wish to make, make it now. And you should not feel at all guilty that its accomplishment was due in part to the unselfish, sincere help of others.

2. — x —   He receives ten pairs of tortoise shells
            whose oracles are irreversible.
            Even the king should use them
            at the sacrifice.
            Doubly auspicious
            if you keep to your course.

There is opposition to someone's generosity toward you. As long
as your relationship with your benefactor does not change, this
opposition will remain ineffectual.

3. — x —   The good man is increased by what is evil.
            His goodness increases.
            He sincerely follows the golden mean:
            it is his badge.
            No guilt.

This is the line of the good Samaritan. An unfortunate occurrence that has brought great trouble to others has given you the
opportunity to help—to comfort, to mitigate pain and hopelessness, to bring the incident to the notice of others who can provide
further aid. Contingent to your generous act are certain rewards: tokens of gratitude and perhaps even public recognition of
your generosity. Do not worry that you have taken advantage of
someone else's misfortune in order to better yourself. Your original generosity was truly generous and not motivated by expectations of your subsequent good fortune.

4. — x —   The man keeps to the mean.
            The prince follows his advice.
            He can be relied on for important things,
            even relocating the capital.

You have a direct and sympathetic relationship with someone
both truly generous and possessed of the means to express his
generosity in many places and in many ways. You have become a
kind of consultant and adviser to this person. He trusts you
because you recognize and appreciate his generosity, yet would
never stoop to taking advantage of it. You are called on to aid him
in a major undertaking. Do not be frightened by the respon-

sibility. You must fulfill this relationship completely to fulfill the Tao of this line.

5. ——o—— The man sincerely seeks to benefit others.
          Others sincerely appreciate him.
          Very auspicious.
          There is no question about it.

You are the generous benefactor of this hexagram. In the path of Artha you are the humanitarian; in the path of kama you have the generous qualities ascribed to Friend; in the path of moksha you are the inspiration for others who follow a path of self-sacrifice. Give fully, without making distinctions, without making judgments, and without reservations.

6. ——o—— No one will support him.
          Everything goes against him.
          His sympathies are fickle.
          Ominous.

Although you have extremely generous principles, you consider yourself on too elevated a plane to act on them in the everyday world. By this neurotic attitude you deny your own natural impulses. You incur the resentment and wrath of others, who can detect your generous impulses and are disappointed when you do not act on them.

43

 Kway · Breakthrough

*Heaven
below*

*The Marsh
above*

ORACLE

The marsh above heaven.
The superior man rains benefits
on those below him,
and does not let his gifts go unused.

*You must expose the matter
in the halls of government,
sincerely and earnestly.
Danger and difficulty.
Announce it to your own city,
but do not call for arms.
Improvement
whatever you do.*

INTERPRETATION

A r t h a ▪ You are threatened by forces opposed to your
principles. For the moment these forces have been diverted and
the threat is minimal, at an ebb. Take advantage of this weakness
both to protect yourself and to exert your own influence on your
adversaries. To best take advantage of this time in which for a
while, the threatening force is weaker than your opposition to it:
(1) Remain resolute and unwavering both in your actions and
principles. (2) Do not keep your anxieties to yourself; express

them to your friends. (3) Do not keep your plans to yourself or prevaricate about your intentions or motives, even though this may seem to expose you somewhat to the forces threatening you. (4) Anyone who might conceivably help you should be included in your efforts. (5) Remain nonviolent. The forces you oppose are the forces of violence. If you, in turn, use violence, you may consider yourself already defeated by them, already under their sway. Be intensely, constantly active and militant in promoting whatever nonviolent plans you have made. A clearly liberal political statement is made in the oracle. In the balance of the universe, the balance between Yin and Yang, all gathering is followed by dispersion. If a man accumulates excessive wealth he must expect an equally excessive dispersion when his finances collapse. The oracle recommends a continuous, gradual dispersion of wealth as it accumulates, as a kind of political and economic safety valve.

K a m a ▪ A pernicious disruptive force has been causing conflict and many unpleasant moments for you and Friend. Because of this selfish, perhaps secret pressure you and Friend have not been completely honest with one another. But the impulse is now at its low point. With love and total sincerity you can break its hold on you. The time has come for you to abandon your separate defenses and communicate frankly to each other—and not only with words—in a mutual effort to overcome the force that threatens your relationship. With honesty and resoluteness you can take advantage of this difficult time to begin to establish a selfless, mutually responsive relationship.

M o k s h a ▪ For one seriously concerned with his spiritual progress it is relatively easy to be rid of the great majority of popular, cultural illusions: e.g., the concept of race, the value of accumulation, the concept of possession, and most dualisms, including the concepts of life and death, good and evil, and mind and body. You may well have reached this point. But your path is now blocked by illusions more difficult to destroy, illusions that have brought you to the point of self-contradiction: the illusion of the value of enlightenment; the illusion of your own selfhood; the illusion that words have meaning; the illusions of space and time, form and history; the illusion of logic. Complete enlightenment occurs when one breaks through *these* illusions. For one reason or another, these illusions are very fragile in you just now. If you apply yourself to whatever spiritual practice you have set for yourself, you may reach your sought-for goal . . . only after you have ceased seeking it, of course.

L I N E S

1. —o— The man walks to the flood on tiptoe.
   Guilt
   and no success
   if you advance.

Instead of efficiently taking advantage of their present weakness, you are unnecessarily mincing in your approach to the forces threatening you. This makes you as weak or weaker than they are. You are not equal to the task of holding them back. To attempt to do so would involve others, as well as yourself, in failure.

2. —o— The man is apprehensive.
   He pleads for help.
   The flood rises in the middle of the night,
   but it will be controlled.

You are wary of any infringements on you or your activities. As long as you remain on your guard, you need not fear any activities of your opponents. You are able to anticipate and effectively meet any move against you.

3. —o— The man is determined to control the flood.
   He is impatient and sets off to meet it by himself.
   When the flood strikes he is not there to give aid.
   For a while, the man is hated;
   eventually people take a more understanding
   attitude.

Circumstances have made you a part and function of the threatening forces you inwardly oppose. Although your sympathies lie entirely with the opposition to these forces, others who also oppose them regard you as an enemy. This is a heartbreaking situation for you; yet you must live with it for a while. If you openly change sides you will alert the threatening force to its weakness. If you remain in your place, without tipping your hand, yet without partaking of any activity against your own principles, you can weaken the threat from within. The breakthrough to be made against the oppressive structure depends on a weakness in the structure. You yourself are that central, telling, undetected weakness. You must grit your teeth and hold on, even though those whom you secretly support attack you and vilify you.

4. ——o—— The flood has flayed the skin from his buttocks.
　　　　　The man can hardly walk.
　　　　　If he becomes sheeplike he will be able to bear
　　　　　his shame.
　　　　　But he is deaf to these words.

You are obstinate and willful. You believe you are omnipotent. In reality you are weak, because you recognize no limits to your activity. You insist on pressing forward although it means getting mired more and more in difficulties. The irony is that if this oracle applies to you, you will not heed it. If you *do* heed it, it does not fit and there is no need to heed it in the first place.

5. ——o—— Keeping the garden weeded
　　　　　requires determined vigilance.
　　　　　The man staves off mistakes and guilt
　　　　　by staying in the center.

The struggle against selfish and unprincipled social forces can be likened to the farmer's struggle against weeds. Neither struggle ever ends. In the same way that weeds are a product of noncultivated soil, evil activity is the product of nonprincipled social standards. The farmer's major effort is the cultivation of vegetables, not the destruction of weeds. He destroys weeds incidentally, only where they inhibit cultivation. Be like a farmer. Learn to live with the weeds; learn to live with evil—don't waste your psyche and strength in attacking it directly. Instead, immerse yourself in the growth and development of positive social principles. As these take hold they will isolate, overwhelm, and finally replace the evil. The phrase "staying in the center" refers to the way one must weed a garden. The farmer walks prudently between the rows of his crop, taking care not to damage its roots with his hoe. When you are ready to destroy the remains of evil, be careful not to harm any principled, benevolent elements that may be intertwined with them.

6. — x — There is no one he can call on.
       Ominous.

You thought you had effectively dispelled the oppressive forces in your life. You relaxed your guard. Now they are back in all their evil glory. Everything has come to naught.

44

Kaou ▪ Temptation

The Wind
below

Heaven
above

O R A C L E

The wind blows beneath heaven.
The prince shouts his orders
and makes his pronouncements
to the four winds.

A strong and willful woman;
do not embrace her.

I N T E R P R E T A T I O N

A r t h a ▪ Your attitude is generally "I can take it or leave it"—and you usually get it without trying. What others devote their lives to achieving often falls into your lap. You claim that you attach no importance to these happy accidents. But beware: you are being subtly seduced. You *have* become attached to your gratuitous success. Instead of simply enjoying the positive aspects of your good fortune you worry about its negative side— the threat of its nonexistence. Instead of remaining cavalier— "Easy come, easy go"—you are haunted by fears of losing what you have so effortlessly, undeservedly gained.

K a m a ▪ You behave as if you are a free agent. In truth you are enslaved by Friend. This is a deception that fulfills a neurotic need in either one or both of you. Deception and dishonesty in the emotions of a relationship, even if tacitly agreed to by both people, keep the relationship from becoming a close one of love and unselfish passion. You are pretending to be your own master, easy and free of excessive attachments. Actually you live and die at Friend's subtle commands. Acknowledge the reality of your total dependence and demonstrate it, not only to F_iend, but to the world, by what you say and what you do.

M o k s h a ▪ This is the hexagram of King Lear. The traditional interpretation of the hexagram is based on the idea that the prince of the oracle has the power to control his subjects from a great distance. But the prince who shouts his commands into the wind is acting absurdly—like Lear, he is mad. To be without humility toward other men is misguided and egotistical; to be without humility toward heaven is purely and simply derangement. For you to believe you can will your own enlightenment is arrogant and patently absurd. You cannot will time to cease; you can only submit and join the dance where there is no time. You cannot will the Yin processes of generation and decay to halt or reverse; you can only submit and lose yourself in the beauty of the process, in which every instance of decay is one of regeneration as well. You cannot will the happiness and peace of an enlightened mind to overwhelm you; you can only submit to the darkness; then, totally lost, you will recognize that you are already happy, at peace, and enlightened.

L I N E S

1. — x — The man should be stymied
     like a carriage both braked and tied.
     Otherwise he is like a lean pig
     trampling around.
     Auspicious
     if you keep to your course.
     Ominous
     if you move in any direction.

The pleasure that drives you needs a strong, consistent check. Your hunger is like the hunger of a lean pig—dangerous and difficult to restrain.

2. —o— The man has a basket of fish.
　　　　　He should not approach the guests.
　　　　　No mistakes.

You protect those close to you from the effects of the cruel pleasures that enslave you. Although trapped and defeated by illusions of your own mind, you need feel no guilt, for you have taken pains to ensure that no one is hurt but yourself.

3. —o— His buttocks have been flayed,
　　　　　and he walks with difficulty.
　　　　　Peril
　　　　　but no mistakes.

You feel like completely giving in to the pleasure that is seducing you, entrapping you. Do not. You can bolster your defenses by imagining how others would see your capitulation to temptation. You can overcome your unreasonable inclinations with an acute fear of embarrassment. As long as you maintain your sense of humor, no disasters will occur.

4. —o— The man has his basket,
　　　　　but there are no fish in it.
　　　　　Ominous.

You have given yourself completely to the pleasures that seduced and ensnared you. Now they have begun to fade and withdraw. Having given yourself to them, when they do depart, what will be left?

5. —o— The medlar tree throws a shadow
　　　　　on the gourd beneath it.
　　　　　If he keeps his brilliance concealed,
　　　　　Heaven will reward him with success.

A melon is delicious, but spoils easily: like the seductive pleasures that give this hexagram its character. You know how to keep your pleasures fresh: although a slave to them, you never tire of them, you are constantly fulfilled by them. Like *any* true and complete union, such an enslavement, such a fulfillment, such an unremitting passion can lead to enlightenment and the highest good.

6. ——o—— He greets everyone
with his horns.
Regrets,
but no mistakes.

You have completely vanquished the tendencies that were endangering you. To others, who saw the source of your temptation as a trifle, weak and defenseless, your violence toward it seems brutal, coarse, and unfair. To those who lack your understanding of the situation your destructive action seems uncalled for. You are despised and humiliated for what seems to be your murderous overreaction. You understand, though, that you had no other choice. You have done what had to be done.

45

Tzhwee ▪ Accord

*The Earth
below*

*The Marsh
above*

O R A C L E

The marsh has risen over the earth.
The superior man puts his weapons in order
and prepares for unforeseen emergencies.

Confer with the great man.
Success
if you keep to your course,
as long as you are willing to pay the price.
Auspicious
no matter what you do.

I N T E R P R E T A T I O N

A r t h a ▪ By design or by chance, happily or unhappily,
you lead most of your life within the limits of a close-knit social
group. This could range anywhere from a close and structured
family situation to a business affiliation or to an idealistic and
demanding political organization. The harmoniousness of the
association depends on the strength of the person at its center.
The Western conceptualization of this person is "leader"; but the
Eastern conceptualization is "he at the center." Understanding
the latter image will help you readjust your relationships within
the group. You will discover the true source of the cohesive force

of your association. A strong center radiates a harmonious group. A weak center is surrounded by discord. If problems have arisen in the context of a concordant group, bring them immediately to the attention of the person at the center. If problems have arisen in the context of a discordant group, the center must be strengthened before the problems can be solved. Acquaint your associates with the difference between the Western "leader" and the Eastern "center man." Associate yourself with the true central force and devote yourself to strengthening it.

K a m a ▪ Your love is based very much on both your and Friend's allegiance to a close-knit, omnipresent group. It could be a political party or a joint artistic endeavor that is the source of the sympathy between you. It could be the family you have raised. Or it could be the separate entity of the two of you together, as friends and/or lovers, that has taken on a special importance for you. Your relationship is just as much a separate, social entity as a government or a rock-and-roll band. Your own relationship will improve as you both accept your relationship to the group, whatever it is. Look to whomever is at the the center of it for guidance. If it is a group of two, look for the center among the experiences and principles you share.

M o k s h a ▪ Some ways of enlightenment encourage isolation and withdrawal as part of their methods. But the path you have chosen—or the path that is right for you—has as its basis community devotion and a communal spiritual sympathy. You are wrong if you believe that you can become spiritually enlightened and yet remain withdrawn from others who have been similarly enlightened. If you do not immediately feel sympathy for *others close to you*, you are a long way from losing your ego enough to regard *all men* as your brothers. Approach whatever is your rightful temple with humility and let yourself be carried away by the anthems of your fellow disciples.

L I N E S

1. — × — Accord desired but impossible to bring about;
   this causes discord.
   The man cries loudly;
   an ally hears him;
   he is soon smiling quietly.
   Advance
   without mistakes
   if you can bear your present difficulties.

Whoever is at the center of your group is unquestionably the strongest, most principled, and most loyal member. Anything that occurs among the other members of the group, outside his knowledge, is not truly representative because he, at the center, is not involved. Everything within the group should go to him and emanate from him. Bring your problem to him and the appropriate resolution will come wisely and naturally from him.

2. — × — Accord achieved through following.
   The man is led by his ally.
   Auspicious
   if you are straightforward.
   The smallest favor is appreciated.

You feel mysteriously drawn to certain relationships and associations which puzzle, perplex, and even frighten you. You are under the influence of the force of a general cultural flux that is reorganizing roles within the society and community. Do not deny your Tao by clinging to traditional concepts of yourself and the universe. The times are changing. And you are part of them.

3. — × — Striving for accord until he is breathless.
   Sighing, the man strives in vain.
   Advance
   without mistakes,
   although you may regret it slightly.

You are an outsider and you want to be an insider. As long as you cling to the outside you will be outside. Only by going inside— toward the center—can you be inside.

4. —o— Accord approaches.
   Very auspicious.
   No one will resent it.
   No blame.

You are a valuable member of the group, with all the miseries and joys that entails.

5. —o— Accord achieved by leading.
   It is organized by the man himself.
   He changes the minds of doubters
   by living continuously in its spirit.
   No mistakes.
   Be firm.
   Guilt disappears.

You think you have friends and associates who have ulterior motives. Do not break off with them. Approach them with an honest and open display of your anxieties.

6. —x— Tearful accord.
   No mistakes.

Express your sorrow. How else can your friends, who can comfort you, know you need comfort?

46

Sheng ▪ Pushing Upward

The Wind
below

The Earth
above

O R A C L E

The trees rise from the earth.
The superior man attends to himself
and takes advantage of minor developments
to achieve an important position.
He advances toward the warmth of friendly ground.

Success.
You may confer with the great man
without fear.

I N T E R P R E T A T I O N

A r t h a ▪ This is the hexagram of the intelligent, responsive, constructive use of your will: neither irrational will used as a battering ram against closed possibilities nor a stubborn will, raised like a dam against irresistible change. You know how to move deliberately and consciously in accord with the movement of changes that occur around you. Nothing you want to happen is going to happen automatically—you must make an effort to achieve it. You must act deliberately and deliberately make the proper connections for your purposes. Your purposes fortunately are in harmony with the general trends of your immediate circle and the culture at large as well. You have an intelligent will.

Whatever efforts you make fit the effortless, will-less pattern of the universal flux.

K a m a ▪ In most love relationships the presence of an active will is disruptive and dangerous. Willfulness that arises from disappointment or from pure selfishness detracts from love. But your willfullness is unselfish and in harmony with the realities of your own and Friend's personalities. Recognize the potential for love in your relationship and consciously, deliberately, dynamically apply yourself to its realization. Because of the unselfishness of your aims, Friend will not feel put upon or threatened by your strong will. Friend will feel bolstered, content, loved because of it.

M o k s h a ▪ A sign of enlightenment is the ability to be spontaneously, thoughtlessly, naturally in tune with the present moment. In order to attain such enlightenment you must apply yourself diligently and with great effort to your spiritual practice. Divine Grace will not descend and sweep *you* away in Its radiant chariot. Your spiritual path seems tedious in a culture that values economy, boring in a culture that values novelty, limiting in a culture that values personal freedom—but at the path's end all such labels lose their meaning. Your spiritual practice is most demanding, but with enlightenment all activities and difficulties resolve themselves. Your enlightenment requires an effort of will: an effort of rigorous asceticism, or an effort at self-deprecating humane and charitable activity, or an effort to communicate with the wise.

L I N E S

1. — x — The climber is welcome.
   Very auspicious.

Your present position is low and humble compared with the position you wish to attain. Your efforts bring out a good-humored, paternal response from those above you. This will result in good luck far above your present expectations.

2. ——o—— The climber's smallest sacrifice
is appreciated.
No mistakes.

You are still far from your goal. You have only meager means and limited resources to support you in your efforts. Since your difficult position is obvious to all, those above you will condescend to accept much less from you than they are accustomed to receive.

3. ——o—— The man climbs up into the empty city.

You must make an effort in order to achieve your aims. But instead of applying yourself to the most direct method for that achievement, you have simply taken the line of least resistance. Instead of dealing with the obstacles that lie naturally in your way, you simply have ignored them and have taken the path that seems to present the fewest obstacles. You have made sure that you have your way in everything you do: but whatever you do gets you nowhere.

4. ——x—— The climber is employed by the king
to present his offerings on Mount Ch'i.
Auspicious.
No mistakes.

You are a member of an elite, honored group of people. As a member of this group you have great influence on the people and events around you. You occupy a special place recognized by all.

5. ——x—— The man climbs the stairs
with dignity.
Auspicious
if you keep to your course.

This is the image of coronation. You are in the position of being a few steps away from reaching crowning honors. As you approach your goal, as your success becomes more and more assured, you may feel impelled to leap the last few remaining steps and possess now what obviously soon will be yours. But it is *not yours yet*. It is yours only in the future. And the future is a figment of your imagination. Continue your normal, balanced efforts.

6. — x — The man climbs blindly.
  Auspicious
  if you keep to your course
  without a single misstep.

You are ambitious, but without goals. You push forward compulsively, blindly. All right: as long as you remain persistent, dynamic, and responsive. All right: as long as you do not look back or wonder where you are going.

47

Khwen · Repression

*The Deep
below*

*The Marsh
above*

O R A C L E

The marsh drains into the deep.
The superior man will make the supreme sacrifice
in the pursuit of his purpose.

Success.
Auspicious
if you keep to your course.
No mistakes.
Make no promises.

I N T E R P R E T A T I O N

A r t h a ▪ The water has drained from the marsh. The
marsh is dry and dead. The water that has drained from the
marsh retains its essential nature, which is to seek its own level.
Without water, however, the marsh loses its essential nature; it is
no longer a marsh. Think of yourself as the solid matter of the
marsh, the flora and the earth of the marsh basin, and the events
of your life as the water, which should fill your form and give it its
essential nature. However, your thoughts and actions, your daily
routine, your cares and joys are being wasted, dissipated, as they
slip through the demands of an illusionary world: the world
of things to cling to and people who cling. You are intimately
involved in the acquisitive struggle, putting an absolute trust in

the value of possession. When you look about you, you see an array of "things" whose most important quality—to you—is a ratio between their desirability and their obtainability. Their desirability you gauge by a system devised by their present possessors. Their obtainability is expressed in dollars and cents. When their desirability exceeds their price you buy them. When their price exceeds their desirability you struggle for them. You are ensnared and confined by this system. In rare instances a person can fully enter this world, knowing it for the illusion it is, treating all its complicated machinations and confrontations as a game. But if you are deeply, seriously, emotionally involved with this acquisitive activity and regard it as the beginning and end of your true fulfillment you will only find yourself trapped on an accelerating treadmill.

K a m a ▪ "Love is a business. If I love you, you must love me. If you do not love me, I will not love you. Here, I give you this much love, now you must give me so much in return. Thank you. Please, I have some love here for you and if you will agree to give me some in return then we can both have the pleasure of being loved. It is very nice love, very good—I can guarantee that you can not find better. I love you very, very much. How much? Not as much as that. I am unhappy because I love you this much and you love me only this much. I envy you because you get so much very nice love from me, so much more and so much better than the love I get from you. It is unfair. Love is a business. But the yogi loves selflessly and neither expects nor demands anything in return." (Paraphrased from a lecture, Swami Satchidananda, Poughkeepsie, New York, March 3, 1970.)

M o k s h a ▪ You have been cut off from all access to a spiritual life. Wherever you turn you find bad karma. When you follow others for spiritual guidance you inevitably discover them to be corrupt and grasping. When you attempt to clear your own mind of its interest in the material world you only rearrange the myriad attachments that bind you and oppress you. There is no relief in sight.

L I N E S

1. — x — Confined beneath a fallen tree
      in a dark valley
      for three years.

You realize that you will never achieve what you desire in the
material world. You have ceased all activity, allowing yourself to
stagnate in despair, cynicism, and self-hate. You have not yet
discovered that the desires unfulfilled and the achievements that
seem unattainable are spurious, corrupt concepts and do not
relate at all to you as an individual, or to your Tao. The powerful
purveyors of a corrupt value system keep you from experiencing
this liberating revelation.

2. — o — Confined at the dinner table.
      When the authorities come
      he remains pious and respectful.
      Ominous
      if you take the initiative;
      but without blame.

Although you are able to provide yourself with all the necessities
of life, you have a chance to acquire more goods and power by
submitting to the authority of someone rich and powerful. There
are initially many drawbacks to this—competitiveness, mistrust, a lack of candor between you. These differences must be
settled and the arrangement entered into in an accepting and
grateful spirit by both parties.

3. — x — Confined by a rock,
      the man grasps at briers.
      In his palace,
      he does not see his wife.
      Ominous.

You deliberately search out obstacles to detain you and complications to entangle you. If you cannot find any you invent them. The
traditional interpretation holds that the man does not see his

wife because she has died while he is busily embroiled in his self-made entanglements. Rather, in his palace, which should be a place of sanctuary, with his perverse tendency to make his own life miserable, he does not recognize his one real source of comfort and solace—his wife.

4. —o— Confined in chrome
in a slow procession.
Some regrets.
Auspicious
in the end.

Material success places you in a circle where the principles and values of your companions inhibit your own progressive and democratic impulses. You are not completely thwarted in your activities. They are simply complicated by humiliating concessions you must make on every hand.

5. —o— Confined by traitors.
His nose and feet are cut off.
He takes it calmly
and accepts his fate.
He remains pious and respectful.

You are so unselfish, so generous that you are considered as an enemy by the selfish, acquisitive forces that surround you. Those who *sell* oppose you because your freehanded generosity makes it look as though what they sell is worthless. Those who *buy* oppose you because your distaste for material goods makes it look as though what they buy is worthless. Ordinarily you could look to the law for relief, but in this case, those who administer the law are prejudiced against you from the start.

6. —x— Confined by ivy
on the edge of the cliff.
He tells himself, "If I move I will regret it."
Repent what has gone before,
then act.
Auspicious.

You want to make a move, make a change. But you feel entrapped and endangered by outside forces. Your fears are groundless. Your oppressors' power has been on the wane for some time. As soon as you *do* what you are determined to do, external pressures will melt and will have no hold on you.

48

Tzhing ▪ The Well

The Wind
below

The Deep
above

O R A C L E

The deep has been contained with wood
and made into a well.
The plan of a town may change
but the location of its wells remains.
The water in the well never disappears
and never increases greatly.
It served those who came before;
it will serve those who come after.
The superior man comforts the people
and stimulates a sense of community.

Ominous
if the rope breaks
before the water is drawn.

I N T E R P R E T A T I O N

A r t h a ▪ When dealing with other people use your
knowledge of human nature to discover their real needs and real
prejudices. You have had much experience in different places and
different social situations. The element common to all is represented by "The Well" of this hexagram: it is the well of human
nature, eternal and ubiquitous in all men. To be able to draw from
your knowledge of essential man is to be in touch with a universal

force. Trust your judgment if it is based on your previous experience with people. There are two dangers in this course. First, there is a danger that you have not followed your insights to their roots and instead have gotten caught up in generalizations on human behavior. You act on precepts, instead of reacting flexibly, appropriately to each different situation. The second danger is of getting too involved in your relations with others and losing sight of your own course. You have a bent toward intuitive sociology; you can trust your judgments about human behavior: but be careful not to get caught up in one concept or theory. Do not let your intuitions lose their still and passive, well-liked nature. Draw from them when you need them, but do not let them propel you into impulsive action.

K a m a ▪ Although Friend is an individual, very special, the only one, do not be reluctant to admit that at a deep level there are similarities between Friend and Friend's predecessors. The well of human nature is omnipresent, even in lovers. It could be that in neglecting this fact and placing Friend above human nature you have been unkind and have denied what, to Friend, is a very real personal property: Friend's humanness.

M o k s h a ▪ Your vision of man is similar to Aristotle's: you see him as a political animal. The peace sought in the way of moksha is not within social bounds, but in your case the path to this peace is through a sympathetic immersion in the social process. The well of human nature is in you too. If you can intuit the truth about yourself you will realize your brotherhood with all men. This realization of brotherhood, fostered by your democratic principles, can become a religious experience. The ultimate end of the concept of brotherhood is an aware denial of the ego. Beware of dogmatism. Beware of falsifying your sympathies.

L I N E S

1. — × — The water is so muddy
          no one will drink it.
          The well is so old
          no creature will use it.

You are too involved with your sympathy for others. You have lost your individuality. You feel for everyone. No one feels for you. No one notices you.

2. — o — There is a leak in the well.
          The bucket is leaky.
          The insects and worms are refreshed.

You are able to sympathize with others, but you do not bother. You have withdrawn and associate only with those whose feelings you can manipulate.

3. — o — The well has been cleared
          but no one uses it.
          Unfortunate, because the water is pure.
          If the authorities came to see,
          all could benefit from it.

You are available to aid someone, but he has not recognized it yet. You are a well of experience from which he could draw; instead, he ignores you. Your friends know you can help him, but they do not want to get involved.

4. — × — The well is well lined.
          No mistakes.

Take care of yourself. Do nothing for others.

5. — o — The water in the well
          is fresh and limpid.
          The man drinks from its cool spring.

Another's mind and heart are open to you. The other needs only an invitation to come and bring about the resolution of all your confusion. But—you do not know who this other is.

6. — x — The well is not allowed to be covered.
The man can always draw water from it.
Very auspicious
if you are sincere.

You do not limit yourself in your sympathies. You see the essential human nature of all men, of all types. This openness brings you joy.

49

Ko · **Revolution**

The Sun
below

The Marsh
above

O R A C L E

A fire within the marsh
The superior man casts
the positions of the stars
and makes clear the seasons and times.

Everyone believes in it
when it is accomplished.
Success.
Keep to your course
and guilt will disappear.

I N T E R P R E T A T I O N

A r t h a · Change is eternal and relentless. When life seems stable, static, and unchanging, the changes taking place are on levels that aren't part of the structure of form and idea that we call "the real world": such changes relate to us and involve us, but we cannot perceive or define them. True oracles are perceptions of these otherwise unknowable changes, perceptions achieved through a religious experience of the totality and unity of the One and All. You wish freely and naturally to move with the changes that influence you, but you are caught up in ambiguities, paradoxes, and culs-de-sac. You feel that the real

world intrudes on your understanding of the present change.
But you do not need oracles or magic to decipher what is going
on. The flux of universal change is manifesting itself in the level
of existence that *is* the so-called "real world." The changes you
wish divulged by the I Ching are clearly visible in the world
about you. Whatever your question is, whatever your problem,
the solution can be found in the changes occurring in the everyday world. Do not resist these changes. Do not ignore them or
consider yourself above them. Do not regard the present upheaval as only an irrelevant game. Revolution *is* a game—of
course—so is acting out every verbalized concept. But at this
time this game is not irrelevant—it is a direct, present manifestation of the Universal flux. You must join it, accept it, be it.
Imagine a ripple in the universe and, as a solitary cork, bobbing
in the void, the so-called "real world." The ripple has met the
cork. The wave of the future is no more; the wave is now. You
are in it. If you try to remain stable on what seems to you to be
solid, you will lose your balance. If you accept the present
disruption for the valid, creative force it is, then you will find
that you naturally adapt to it and the solution to your problem
will occur spontaneously.

K a m a ▪ Conflicts between you and Friend are caused by a
change in your relationship. Both of you are resisting this
change, clinging to your roles and values of the immediate past.
It is true that the previous structure of your relationship—the
balance of give and take, dominance and submissiveness, liber-
ties and responsibilities, that existed until recently—was a comfortable one, in which loving was very easy. But changes are
inevitable and they have occurred. You must go along with them.
Look at your relationship with a fresh eye. Forget about past
resolutions to past conflicts. Accept these changes and the new
roles and new levels of communication they call for. You and
Friend will naturally adjust to them. If you cannot accept them,
then it is better not to cling to past joys, but realistically to accept
the consequences of changes that will keep you constantly divided and in irreconcilable conflict.

M o k s h a ▪ Although enlightenment reduces all forms and concepts to absurdity, any "way of enlightenment," any religion, any spiritual path, originally develops from some experience, some idea—some illusion. This illusion—Buddhahood, the ego, the eternal present, Christ's divinity, etc.—remains valid throughout one's spiritual life—except at the moment of total enlightenment, when even this last illusion is destroyed. In your case, the changes in "the real world," in your environment, in your society, have made themselves felt in your deepest perceptions of the universe, those with which you have formed the divine image that shapes your spiritual life. You no longer fully believe in the validity of that image. You no longer have faith. The world has changed so much that your original experience, the image that has guided you, no longer has the meaning for you that it once had. Enlightenment lies no longer on the path you follow. You must give it up. Do not begin immediately to search for a new philosophy. Let yourself move with the changes that are developing around you. The new spiritual path for you will be revealed naturally through your new conceptions and perceptions of the world, your *new* illusion of experience.

L I N E S

1. —o— He is bound with yellow oxhide.

Yellow is the color of the unchanging and unchangeable abiding golden mean; the ox is the symbol of docility. You are in the midst of change that you can neither anticipate, nor promote, nor influence. Do not try to participate in it. For the time being, let yourself lag behind current trends.

2. —x— In his own time he makes a radical change.
   Auspicious
   if you take action.
   No mistakes.

Consider objectively what effect current changes will have on your personal life. Change your values to reconcile them to the new communal values that will result from the widespread radical change that is taking place. Submit to the influence of a leader in the change; someone whose values seem to be at the center of the change; someone who is important enough to be regarded as one of its symbols.

3. ——o—— When the changes he contemplates
have been fully deliberated three times
he will be trusted.
Ominous
if you take action.
Peril
if you keep to your course.

Besides the deep and inexorable change that is disrupting the structures of the past there is also a false change: a decoy revolution based on past, not future, values. It is a snare set by those still in control to entice you, confuse you, and exploit you. Learn to distinguish between the real revolution and its empty mimic. Otherwise you will remain dependent on concepts and institutions that have no future but to fall apart. Do not participate in any aspect of change without the approval of those you trust.

4. ——o—— *Guilt disappears.*
You are trusted.
Auspicious
if you challenge present institutions.

A successful revolution (within an individual or a group) is one in which the professed values (as opposed to the real values) of the old order are made the real values of the new order.

5. ——o—— He changes boldly
as the tiger changes his stripes.
He is trusted
before he consults the oracle.

You are caught up in the great change that is taking place. You have taken your position. You have committed yourself. You have so fully entered into the emerging of the new world that you have become to others a symbol of change. Your Tao is so clear and so public that it is beyond influence by oracles or by any personal decisions of your own.

6. — x — He changes subtly
like the leopard changes his spots.
Smaller men change their faces
to show obedience.
Ominous
if you advance.
Auspicious
if you keep to your course.

You are reserved and withdrawn. Because of your quiet and uncomplicated philosophy of life, the effect on you of the great changes that are occurring throughout the world will be small and insignificant. This is the line of Marcus Aurelius.

50

Ting · The Caldron

The Wind
below

The Sun
above

O R A C L E

Fire burns over wood.
The superior man tends the fire
and secures the success of the offering.

Great success.

I N T E R P R E T A T I O N

A r t h a ▪ The caldron of this hexagram is specifically a
large bronze vessel used at banquets and for sacrificial offerings.
It symbolizes double good fortune: in the *home* it was a symbol of
material prosperity; the *temple* caldron was a symbol of a happy
humility toward the One and All. The trigram Wind/Wood is
beneath the trigram The Sun/Fire. Wood and fire are in their
proper position. In the same way, your material life is properly
subservient to your spiritual life. You are prosperous. With the
peace of mind that prosperity brings, you can afford to place a
higher value on your spiritual path than on material considerations. You bring to your work the interest and skill it deserves,
but without emotional involvement, without despair or jubila-
tion, neither of which it deserves. Two grand examples of your
Tao would be: a modern Japanese industrialist who daily sits za-
zen; a famous artist who shuns publicity and retains his inner

humility. Although your own life may not be on as public a scale, it is equally content. Your values are admirably placed. Remain unconcerned about your worldly life and you will attain the happy oracles of this hexagram.

K a m a ▪ You and Friend are content, happy with each other and honest in your love. But these pleasurable aspects of your relationship play only a small part in your life together. Together you are preoccupied with your spiritual path. Together you work to attain and maintain a peaceful and reverent way of life. Your complete, undemanding love for each other engenders many spiritual opportunities and insights. Together, you are capable of practicing the rituals of tantra.

M o k s h a ▪ You are a spiritual person who plays a role dedicated to spiritual matters. Unhappily, this combination does not often occur in our culture. A priest who lives in Christ; a guru who ignores his ego; a psychiatrist who loves his patients: these are examples of this kind of excellence.

L I N E S

1. — x — The caldron has been overturned
       in order to cleanse it.
       The concubine gives birth to a son
       and improves her position.
       No mistakes.

It is necessary for you to do something against established principles in order to maintain certain personal principles of your own. There is nothing wrong in this.

2. —o— A stew in the caldron.
       Auspicious
       if you feel safe from your enemies.

You are envied for your prosperity. Because you are a devout and moral person, without feelings of superiority, the resentment of others is harmless.

3. —o— The ears of the caldron
        are not in the right place.
        The man is stopped short.
        The pheasant will remain uneaten.
        The gentle rain will finally bring relief.
        Guilt will disappear.
        Auspicious
        in the end.

When the caldron's handles are inconveniently placed, it cannot be lifted from the fire; the meat within it burns, becoming inedible. Although you are prosperous and generous, you are in a situation where you cannot put your prosperity and good intentions to use. Maintain your inner values, even if you cannot implement them as you wish. Eventually things will change and the atmosphere will be more conducive to your principles.

4. —o— The man breaks the feet of someone else's
        caldron.
        It tips
        and everything spills out.
        Ominous.
        Guilt.

You have been given too great a responsibility. You have neither the personality, nor the experience, nor the strength to fulfill it.

5. —x— The caldron has yellow ears and gold rings.
        Keep to your course.

The caldron with golden handles, although more precious, is not as useful as it could be because it cannot be carried when it is hot. It can be used, but it must be left in its place over the fire. You are too shy to express to others the charity and love you feel. You are generous only when approached. This is your nature. Continue in it.

6. —o— The caldron has handles of jade rings.
   Very auspicious.
   Success,
   whatever you do.

A caldron with jade handles is both precious and useful. The caldron can be carried and passed around among guests when it is hot. You have the ability to actively pursue your humane and generous principles.

51

Khen · The Thunderclap

Thunder
below

Thunder
above

O R A C L E

Thunderclap follows thunderclap.
The superior man is fearful and apprehensive.
He cultivates his good qualities
and examines his faults.

When the thunder comes,
be on your guard,
yet smile and talk cheerfully.
When the thunder terrifies everyone
within a hundred miles,
be like the sincere worshiper
who does not spill a drop of the
sacrificial wine.

I N T E R P R E T A T I O N

A r t h a ▪ This is a time of sudden catastrophic events.
Remain cool. Expect a general reaction of shock and fear and
then hysteria. Do not get caught up in it. If you retain a deep
acceptance of the inevitability of the present moment, then you
will ride out the present widespread catastrophe wiser and stronger than you were before.

K a m a ▪ You and Friend have been struck by an unforeseen and seemingly disastrous event. If you react with selfish anxieties you will start blaming each other for whatever has occurred. If you hysterically fantasize yourselves out of seeing the reality of the catastrophe, it will overcome you. If you remain calm and meet your problems in the same warm and loving spirit with which, up till now, you have met your pleasures, then this disaster can only benefit you in the long run by deepening the bond between you.

M o k s h a ▪ A time of catastrophic "acts of God" is a good time to examine the depth of your spiritual commitment. With an enlightened point of view you have learned to accept the bad moments of your life. You have learned not to grasp possessively at the good moments. You have lived in a state of peace and equanimity. But in the face of the present disasters you are rediscovering fears and anxieties in yourself. Thus you do *not* completely, deeply, effortlessly accept the will of God. You have not thrown off your ego so thoroughly that you can face these times with a Buddhalike calm. It is good that you have discovered this. It points to where you must now strive on your path to *complete* enlightenment.

L I N E S

1. ——o—— The thunderclap draws him to the window.
   Apprehensively he looks around.
   After that he is cheerful and congenial.
   Auspicious.

At first the threat of sudden disaster seems aimed directly at you. You fear that you will bear the brunt of it. When none of these dire consequences occur, the relief you experience will be so great and so liberating that it will put you in a state of mind to achieve great success.

2. — x — The thunderclap endangers him.
   He abandons his belongings
   and ascends to safe heights.
   He need not worry about his possessions.
   In seven days he can reclaim them.

Disaster has struck close to you. You have lost many of your material possessions. If you regard your possessions as so much a part of yourself that you become distraught and hysterical, then you allow the disaster to strike *you* and shatter *you* as well as *your things*. Remain calm in the understanding that the material world is always transitory and subject to sudden changes. You need not suffer. You will soon regain possession of whatever you *need*.

3. — x — The nerve-racking thunderclaps agitate him.
   No mistakes
   if your apprehensions cause you
   to keep to your course.

In your case, a passive reaction to the sudden catastrophe is *not* your proper course. You should not simply let fate take its course. Retaining your presence of mind, act with it. Go with the events. A sense of danger is good here; it is what will spur you to action.

4. — o — The thunderclaps overtake him
   flat on his back in the mud.

You are not resilient enough to ward off the effects of disaster. You are too inflexible to change in accordance with them. You are going to have to live with your unwelcome, unexpected problem for a long time.

5. — x — Amid the thunderclaps
   he goes about his business,
   even though he is in danger;
   otherwise he would suffer a loss.

You are in the midst of tumultuous times, repeated catastrophes, caused by a conflict between two powerful opposing forces over which you have no control and which have no concern for you. The natural reaction is to seek shelter. That is what everyone else has done. But you cannot afford to; there are things you must do. You are involved in affairs that require your immediate action. Brave the storm and carry them through.

6. — x — Amid the thunderclaps
he becomes hysterical.
If he had taken precautions
before the thunder was directly overhead
he would never have made a mistake,
even though members of his family might speak
against him.
Ominous
if you take action.

You recognize an oncoming catastrophe because it has hit others close to you. Withdraw completely from the area in which the disasters are occurring. Do not heed the hysterical anger, spite, and gossip against you that will accompany your withdrawal.

52

Ken ▪ **Keeping Still**

*The Mountain
below*

*The Mountain
above*

O R A C L E

One mountain above another.
The superior man does not let his mind
stray from his immediate activities.
His back is at rest
and he is free from self-consciousness.
He walks about his courtyard
without noticing the people in it.

No mistakes.

I N T E R P R E T A T I O N

N o t e ▪ The spine is the medium between psychological
stress and the tension in the body. If the spine is totally at rest,
the body is totally relaxed. If the spine is *totally* at rest, it
indicates that the mind has overcome that first and primal psychological stress, the illusion of ego, that fosters man's charac-
teristic alienation from the world around him.

A r t h a ▪ Your direction is essentially spiritual. Whatever material problems you have are only shadows of your spiritual struggle. If you perceive a problem, then your problem is

that you perceive it as a problem in the first place: you know better. You understand and have experienced the stillness of this hexagram. The "question" about which you have consulted the I Ching oracle is predicated on concepts and values which *you know* have no substance in a state of keeping still. And keeping still, at rest, at one with time and space, is your Tao.

K a m a ▪ Although you see *your own* anxieties as the absurdities they are, you have let yourself get caught up in *Friend's* anxieties. You accept Friend's seriousness about these anxieties, although they themselves are as absurd as any others. A love relationship is the most difficult illusion to deflate on the spiritual path. An enlightened businessman recognizes the absurdity of business. An enlightened student recognizes the absurdity of scholarship. An enlightened patriot recognizes the absurdity of nationalism. But an enlightened lover does not as easily recognize the absurdity of love. This is not to say that there should be no emotional, loving bond between yourself and Friend. But allow the emotions and the love to well spontaneously from what you are and what you are to each other at the moment. Don't impose a static, illusory, romantic framework on your present moments together.

M o k s h a ▪ You are in the practice of moksha. You are on the path. You will know yourself as neither alive nor dead. Do Hatha-Yoga, or the Japanese physical discipline hara, or another system that regards the body as an animal form of divine principles, instead of a beast of burden for Time.

L I N E S

1. — x — His toes are still.
   No mistakes.
   Keep to your course.

If you feel any hesitation as you are just beginning something, trust in your doubts and change your direction. Before an activity or a relationship has had a chance to solidify into something hard and opaque, you have your purest, truest vision of it. If something seems wrong *now*, it will remain so, even though some polished system of give-and-take eventually obscures it. Trust any negative feelings in your first judgments as a kind of reverse beginner's luck. Careful: your reaction to second thoughts should be a shift of direction, not a reversal, not a pulling back. The impetus for your direction remains valid and you do not fulfill an impetus by quelling it.

2. — x — His calves are still.
　　　　　　He cannot aid the man in front of him
　　　　　　and he feels frustrated.

You are frustrated in your efforts to pass your vision on to others. You know that the ultimate end of their delusions is absurdity, pettiness, and lonely misery. But let it be. There is nothing you can do about it.

3. — o — His haunches are still.
　　　　　　His back is rigid.
　　　　　　The situation is perilous.
　　　　　　Painfully, he stifles his excitement.

You are forcing yourself to act and think in an enlightened way. But an enlightened "way of being" is only another stiff and conventional concept from which you must free yourself. Bodhidharma was irascible, rowdy, and intemperate. Be yourself.

4. — x — His trunk is still.
　　　　　　No mistakes.

You are near to enlightenment. You have achieved a state of rest, physically, emotionally, temporally, but have not yet freed yourself from the thoughts and impulses that make up the structure of your ego.

5. — x — His jaw is relaxed;
     his words are orderly.
     Guilt disappears.

You have a tendency to show off your unconcern about practical problems by treating them lightly, by chattering freely about them, and by exhibiting a generally carefree attitude. This only demonstrates the great depths of your anxieties. If you were truly free of these meaningless problems, you would not adjust your manner to them.

6. — o — He devotes himself
     to remaining at rest.
     Auspicious.

Tranquillity.

53

Khyen ▪ Procession

The Mountain below

The Wind above

O R A C L E

A tree on the mountain.
The superior man maintains his good character
and sets an example for the people.
The young girl celebrates her marriage.

Auspicious.
Keep to your course.

I N T E R P R E T A T I O N

A r t h a ▪ Lead your life in close accord with accepted customs and norms. Trust in the basic justice and efficiency of the social mechanism. Your role in it is marked out clearly. You can be content in it. You know what is expected of you—the socially acceptable, the traditional, the "normal." Do it. Although it is slow, gradual, unexciting, and unchallenging, it is direct, decisive, and sure. Any wavering from your proper course, for which there are many precedents, would be very unwise.

K a m a ▪ You and Friend are both part of a community, or a subculture or an ethnic or religious group, or a similar congregation of people that subscribes to its own traditional mores and customs in courtship and love. Recognize your kinship with this common culture; apply the traditional courtesies and taboos, licenses, and restrictions to your relationship with Friend—not because they have any ultimate, absolute value, but because they are best suited to your own common traditions and values. If you are impatient with these customs, bored or embarrassed by them, and attempt to avoid them, you and Friend will find yourselves in conflict with each other. Your relationship will be strengthened if you plunge together into your common background and follow whatever measures are prescribed for a loving couple within it.

M o k s h a ▪ As a spiritual person you understand that all values are pure illusion, maya, the dust on the mirror. You probably have not freed yourself from *all* such values and concepts, but you have freed yourself from most of them and believe that society could do without them as well. But, although you feel personally free from the social structure, your spiritual path lies within it. There is a place for your nonsocial principles within society. There is a structure of acceptable means of action and communication for you to use in order to slowly but surely bring about the changes you envision.

L I N E S

N o t e ▪ The image of the lines of this hexagram is a flight of migrating geese, an exquisite symbol of gradual progress achieved through a precise and tantamount social order. For man, a socially contradictory and ambivalent animal, the beauty of a formation of wild geese is especially poignant.

1. — x — The wild geese reach the shore.
   The young officer will encounter obstacles.
   There will be talk
   but no mistakes.

The shore of this oracle is the shore of the home lake; it is the point where flight begins. You are just setting out on your path. You have just entered a situation that will involve you totally and influence your activity for a long time. It is still unfamiliar. You have made some mistakes that have drawn criticism from unsympathetic people. But these are not unusual, forgivable mistakes *and* the criticism of them are ultimately good. They will teach you the accepted ways of handling yourself and make you aware of the step-by-step nature of your course.

2. — x — The wild geese reach the boulders
             where they can refresh themselves and rest.
             Auspicious.

Boulders provide a safe resting place at the beginning of flight. Their heights provide vantage points; their irregularities provide protective crannies. But their defensive advantage is only effective for groups. For a single goose boulders would be a somewhat dangerous resting place. If you share your world with others it will be your sanctuary. If you remain alone you invite trouble.

3. — o — The wild geese reach the desert.
             The husband leaves on an expedition,
             but will not return.
             The wife is pregnant
             but will not nurse her child.
             Ominous.
             Defend your interests.

You have not followed the course prescribed for you and, in an attempt to act individualistically, instinctively, and aggressively, you have gotten yourself into a tight and hostile situation. What has been done has been done. It is not possible for you to retrace your steps. Accept your present conditions and fend off your enemies as best you can.

4. — x — The wild geese reach the trees.
             They can alight
             on the broad branches.
             No mistakes.

Unavoidable but quite ordinary circumstances have placed you in an awkward situation. You did not foresee such an occurrence and were totally unprepared for it. You have been thrown off balance; you feel acutely embarrassed. There may be a way you can fit in this situation so that whatever happens in it will not affect you adversely. On the other hand, there may not.

5. —o— The wild geese reach the hill.
   The wife is barren for three years,
   then nothing can stop her.
   Auspicious.

You have progressed so far and so much faster than others that you have become temporarily alienated from your friends and colleagues. You feel lonely and misunderstood, although in your own eyes you have fulfilled yourself. The attitudes of others have changed toward you: some have become spiteful, some shy, some obsequious, and some haughty. But this is only a passing phase. As your new position becomes more established and accepted, your social relationships will return to normal.

6. —o— The wild geese reach the farthest mountains.
   Their feathers can be used as ornaments.
   Auspicious.

This line indicates reaching the ultimate end of your course and leaving it behind for a new one. It is time to abandon your values and change your goal. Turn from the rewards that you have gathered on your way. Leave them as tokens to others; your ultimate achievement and then your transcendence of it makes them meaningful symbols. This oracle indicates an absolute and final break with the past, and a new existence for you.

54

Kway-Mai ▪ The Marrying Maiden

The Marsh
below

Thunder
above

O R A C L E

Thunder over the marsh.
The man who knows the eternity of the end
knows the trials of the beginning.

Ominous.
Action brings failure.

I N T E R P R E T A T I O N

A r t h a ▪ You play a vital but subordinate role in your situation: similar to that of a catalyst in a chemical reaction. The image of the hexagram is (depending on the culture) the concubine, the second wife, or the young mistress of an amenable ménage. Your role is not the result of *your* efforts or of *your* mistakes. You play your part by the grace of those who control the situation. You fulfill certain general requirements of theirs—outside of that, they have little concern for you. You are used, not for what you do, but for what you are. No different from the virgins sacrificed by the Aztecs, you fill your position not because of your personal qualifications, but because you best fit an already established ideal agreed upon by those who have control of the situation. Remain passively, traditionally, what you are. Any forward move, any creative or individualistic act will destroy your image and disappoint your patrons. Besides ancient Chinese concubines and Aztec virgins, this would also be the hexagram, for example, of the bright young executive promoted in order to act as a buffer between rival executives; or of the actress given a role because of her clever new name and the shape of her buttocks; or of the token black scholarship student at a traditionally white school. In all cases the advice is: Don't rock the boat. You are involved in a situation whose varied elements do not really concern you personally, and which you can influence in no way.

K a m a ▪ You are loved by Friend not as you yourself are, but as a symbol or as a means to something else. Friend is attracted to you by something only incidentally yours and not essentially part of you. As a woman you might, for example, have an aristocratic air that attracts Friend or you might respond sexually in a way ideal for Friend or you might resemble his wife or mother. As a man you might attract Friend by your wealth or your social connections or because Friend needs a cheap short-order cook in her diner. If you wish to maintain the relationship with Friend, you need only maintain that which attracts Friend to you. You need not communicate, you need not love, and you had better not surprise.

M o k s h a ▪ Only on the wheel of karma is there inequality; within eternity we are all the same, all One. And even in the maya that binds you the great principles of Yin and Yang create balance in all things. Your spiritual path is one of self-consolation. Trust in the just and even balance of the universe.

L I N E S

1. ──●── The betrothed is not the first
             either in time or preference.
             The lame manage to get along.

*Auspicious
for an advance.*

Someone close to you occupies a position for which you yourself
are better suited. You play an inferior role to this person. Because of your close personal relationship you are in an impossible
bind, with no hope of improvement. However, you are free to act
and move and carry out your essential role to the best of your
ability, without danger or complications arising. The circumstances have another favorable aspect: because all can see the
bind you are in, no one fears or envies you; in fact, everyone goes
out of his way to be helpful.

2. —o— The betrothed is blind in one eye
but she can still see.
The course she keeps to
is like that of a widow.

You are in a relationship where the other parties have disappointed you. Since your judgment is so bad, from now on you had
better avoid similar relationships.

3. —x— The marriage does not please the maiden.
She returns home and accepts her former place.

You are willful and resilient. You have achieved your goal, but
now find that it does not satisfy you. You have backed off. The
outcome is uncertain.

4. —o— The maiden procrastinates.
Sooner or later she will marry.

You hold yourself in high esteem. You have refused offers of
various roles and positions because of the insincere motivations
behind them. It may seem that all chances for an honest and
acceptable position have passed you by. But your perseverance
was correct and the appropriate opening for you will appear in
time.

5. —x— The maiden is not as beautiful as the bridesmaids.
The moon is not yet full.
Auspicious.

By tradition and the social norms you are bound to accept a certain inconsequential role when, by logic and relevance, you are fit to play a more important one. You respect the tradition and therefore accept the minor role without regrets. Waiting will bring good luck.

6. — x — The maiden is barren.
       The groom's knife draws no blood
       from the sheep.
       No improvement.

You cannot fulfill your role as you are expected to do. There is nothing you can do about it.

55

Feng ▪ Abundance

*The Sun
below*

*Thunder
above*

ORACLE

Thunder and lightning:
the height of the storm.
The superior man judges lawsuits
and declares them fairly.

*When the administrator achieves prosperity,
he need not fear replacement.
Be like the sun at noon.
Improvement.*

INTERPRETATION

Artha ▪ The trigrams represent movement (*Chen*, Thunder) and clarity (*Li*, Fire). You have a strong will and the ability to act; you retain your peace of mind and open vision. This combination of attributes has given you the ability both to judge a situation candidly, objectively, and then to act freely and purposefully on your judgment. Because of this double advantage you have easily reached your goal. You now possess what you desired and are free from what oppressed you. But you move because it is in your nature to move; because of your clear, objective vision, your goals are secondary; neither failure nor success makes you pause. The mountaineer who does not cease moving when he reaches the top of the mountain can go in only one direction: down. Do not be surprised if you move away from the goals and ideals which seemed to inspire you. You retain something from your success: material gains or the realization of personal needs—such things as honor, status, and power. But with your clear, unfettered mind you know that possession is an illusion and so is social position. You have achieved what you desired but you have not fulfilled yourself. You are not yet happy. But do not be *un*happy. It is absurd to feel sorrow and sense of loss at the successful conclusion of your worldly ambitions. Be neither happy nor unhappy, just be: be abundant, be full, be now, like the sun at its zenith, in its glory, about to descend.

K a m a ▪ Friend's love for you seems to be everything you've ever wanted from another person. And yet you are not happy. The form of the relationship seems to be a fulfillment of your imagined ideals. But your well-defined desires block Friend's love for you, refract it, filter it. You hold abstract ideals of love; Friend's love for you must pass in review before these ideals. You have set, conceptualized desires; Friend's love for you must undergo judgment in terms of these static prerequisites. The ideals seem fulfilled, the prerequisites seem fulfilled, yet you still cannot experience Friend's love directly, from person to person, from Friend to you. Stop wanting; start having. Knowing how love blossoms and then wanes, you are already experiencing anxiety about the future. Be like the midday sun, the sun at its zenith; it is highest, brightest, most glorious at that point; and it is not the sun which has just risen or the sun which will set—it is the sun now, in an infinitesimal space of time, momentarily tangent to heaven.

M o k s h a ▪ You have reached a peak in your spiritual life. You have studied, practiced rituals, and meditated. You have achieved the clear understanding you desired: you can unify the paradox. But still you wonder where enlightenment is. Now is the time to enter fully into Buddha's stricture: Be without desire. If you desire enlightenment, you are wise enough to know that under conditions of desire enlightenment cannot be attained. It cannot be "attained" in any case; it can only occur. You have solved the paradox. Now abolish the illusion of your own ego. There is no paradox. There is no solution. There is no one to solve it.

L I N E S

1. ——o—— He meets his mate
who is very much like him.
No mistakes.
Approval
if you advance.

A combination of inner clarity and outward movement has brought about your success. You possess only *one* of these qualities. Someone else who possesses the complementary quality shares with you the honors for your present state of abundance. Without the other's clarity of judgment (if you are the energetic one) or without the other's authority and capability for action (if you are the thoughtful one) you could not have attained your mutual good fortune. You must go out of your way to contact this other person. Do not be shy. The other person is aware of the connection between the two of you. He will meet you with recognition and in friendship. You should have a lengthy and fruitful association.

2. —x— The screens are so huge
he can see the Big Dipper at noon.
If he approaches the ruler with the truth
he will encounter suspicion and dislike.
If he can summon up loyalty toward him
the ruler will see the truth.
Auspicious.

You are being willfully and successfully eclipsed by someone. Do not try actively to change this situation—you will meet with mistrust and hatred. Instead, establish a relationship with the one who is eclipsing you. He cannot deny either to himself or you that he has usurped your place. With the help of his feelings of guilt, you and he will be able to work things out—and to your advantage.

3. —o— The screens have been draped with thick curtains.
        He can see small stars at noon.
        In the darkness he breaks his right arm.
        No mistakes.

Your eclipse in this case is so complete, the darkness so thick, that there is nothing you can do. The situation that you brought to a successful conclusion has been taken completely out of your hands. You have no position in it. You have no power over it. You can taste none of the fruits of your success.

4. —o— The tent is so heavy
        he can see the Big Dipper at noon.
        He meets his mate
        who is very much like him.
        Auspicious.

The eclipse is on the wane. You have made contact with your counterpart. (See interpretation of line 1 above.) Together you can create abundance.

5. —x— He gathers around him brilliant men.
        Praise.
        Auspicious.

In the glow of your success the true qualities of those involved with you reveal themselves: you have chosen your associates wisely.

6. —x— He has a large house
        that hides him from view.
        He stares at his door
        but it never opens.
        For three years he sees no one.
        Ominous.

You are so anxious about your newly acquired abundance that you cannot enjoy it. You cannot even see it. All you feel is fear of losing it. All you see are images of its loss. It is farther from you now than ever.

56

Liu · The Stranger

*The Mountain
below*

*The Sun
above*

O R A C L E

Fire on the mountain
The superior man acts
wisely and cautiously;
he has no time for lawsuits.

*Some improvement.
Auspicious
if you keep to your course.*

I N T E R P R E T A T I O N

A r t h a · Your life is an odyssey. You are constantly on
the move from place to place. You find comfort in your sense of
yourself moving. Maybe you are a practical nomad like Hemingway; or an æsthetic nomad like Cocteau; or an intellectual nomad
like Norman O. Brown; or a spiritual nomad like Bishop Pike.
You are always on your way into something or on your way out of
something. This is not an aimless, chancy wandering—it is the
movement of fire on a mountain which travels on an unrelenting
pursuit of its own fuel, a search for its means of continuing
existence. You feed on the best of the different places or ideas or
roles you wander into; when that is consumed you wander out
again. Because of your mercurial character you have very few

acquaintances at any one time, although you have left myriads behind you. This is a bittersweet Tao: bittersweet because the joy of discovery is always paired with the hopelessness of your search. Avoid getting yourself involved in any long-term agreements. Avoid committing yourself to any action in the distant future.

K a m a ▪ Perhaps you are a sexual nomad. Perhaps you wander in and out of relationships, using them and the people involved to give your life meaning. If Friend is similarly inclined, then you will have a short, happy relationship; if Friend has a genuine and deep-set affection for you, then it will be a short, *unhappy* relationship. If Friend is a friend, Friend is bound to be hurt. As for yourself: strangers do not get hurt, they only come and go. Be careful to be honest and sincere with Friend: do not invent emotions you do not feel. If you accept your wanderlust without shame and without fear, it will reveal itself naturally in your relationship; Friend, knowing what to expect, even if eventually disappointed, will not be disillusioned. It is also possible to be an emotional nomad within the bounds of a single extended or permanent love relationship. If Friend is a fellow traveler with you on these excursions into different moods and different needs and different ways of being, then your relationship can be a happy one. If Friend is more static than you then Friend is liable to feel confused, unsure, even neglected—unable to catch up with you as you pass through phase after phase. A realistic, straightforward attitude, and a low-key passion is the best way of love for a stranger such as you.

M o k s h a ▪ Enlightenment for you is not a final revelation. It is never a complete experience. When a specific spiritual path enlightens you, you feel that you must move on. Your spiritual experiences have great meaning for you, but they are always in the past. Once you reach the top of the mountain the only direction—for the wanderer who must keep moving—is down; and then up again, by another route. In your travels up and down the spiritual mountain you resemble Sisyphus. But while Sisyphus is bent with despair at his hopeless labor, you are erect and hopeful in your quixotic meanderings. Your fickleness may lead you into extreme, esoteric, unexplored spiritual systems.

L I N E S

1. — × — A petty stranger
       with petty motives.
       Further calamity.

Someone who is deeply and permanently involved in a situation can view it in many ways and treat it with differing degrees of seriousness and cynicism. You, however—always a transient— have no right to treat lightly what are to others serious matters. A cavalier, offhand attitude on your part is out of place and would be resented. It is an invitation to disaster.

2. — × — A well-to-do stranger
       has come to town.
       He stays at the inn
       with his loyal retinue.

Although a wanderer, you have a clear and unvarying strong sense of yourself: a philosophical center. You are your own quiet and restful place that you bring with you wherever you go. Others, without such a center, are drawn to you.

3. — o — The stranger has burned down the inn,
       and has been deserted by his friends.
       Peril,
       even while you keep to your course.

You have become emotionally involved in a situation. You have lost yourself in the ideas and conflicts of the moment. Because you are a traveler you elicit no sympathy from others. It takes time to turn acquaintances into friends.

4. — o — A wandering woodcutter has settled here.
       He makes a good living
       but seems uneasy about something.

The nature of your true fulfillment is wandering. But you have ceased to wander. You have found a comfortable niche and have allowed yourself to fit into it. You are involved in activities and plans that deny your restless nature.

5. —×— The stranger shoots the pheasant.
       He exchanges his arrow for praise
       and a position of responsibility.

Accept the forms and courtesies of whatever situation you are in. Appreciate their connection with universal principles—even though they are otherwise foreign and meaningless to you.

6. —o— The stranger kindles his fire with a bird's nest.
       This gives joy to the fire
       but undermines the man.
       He loses his composure.
       Ominous.

In your unrelenting and vigorous motion you resemble fire on a mountain. You are like such a fire brightly flaring as it engulfs the reedy, dry bird's nest. You experience great joy as you are invigorated at the expense of something rare and fragile and of value to others. By your heedless, irremediable act of destruction, you have lost what was once your most valuable quality: gentle respect for the values of others.

57

Sun • The Penetration of the Wind

The Wind
below

The Wind
above

O R A C L E

Two winds penetrate
into every nook and cranny.
The superior man reaffirms his orders
and secures his activities.

Some improvement
especially if you keep moving
with some direction in mind.
Confer with the great man.

I N T E R P R E T A T I O N

A r t h a • This is the hexagram of the subtle penetration of the wind. Remain in the background; take no direct action. Allow the force of your character to influence the situation, unhindered by your will and ego. To attempt actively to force the situation would be simply to dissipate your energies. To willfully apply your own wants and needs to the situation would be to become dependent on the situation instead of an influence on it—part of the problem instead of part of the solution. These dangers are most imminent when your personal welfare is most at stake. Try not to get emotionally involved in what is happening around you.

K a m a ▪ Open yourself to the quiet penetration of Friend's character. And do not try to impress your own character on Friend. Love and will are antitheses. By the open acceptance of each other's personality—peculiarities and all—you can begin to get to know each other. This is a hexagram of an unemotional way of loving. If you are neurotic, in your love life whatever emotions you feel will be egotistical, willful, perhaps even offensive—expressions of such emotions are not expressions of selfless love. Wait, instead, until you can express the emotion of egoless joy which will arise from a mutual openness and sympathy.

M o k s h a ▪ You understand that your day-to-day experiences are maya, illusion. But they seem to clutter your life. They keep you from the spiritual peace you seek. You want suddenly to break through, into the clear. You systematically try different intellectual tricks to reason your way into paradise. But it is not only the things and events in your life that are illusion, but also *the separation* you make *between yourself and them.* You *are* in the clear *already.* Trust your understanding, your deep, wordless understanding, and do not trouble about the exteriors of things any further. A quiet penetration of each other by you and "it" can take place as the illusionary boundaries that define "you" dissolve into unity and peace.

L I N E S

1. — x — He comes and goes
   like little gusts of wind.
   Keep to your course
   like a brave soldier.

Be careful that your quiet reticence does not lead to indecisiveness. Behind your inoffensive, withdrawn attitude should lie strong and unyielding resolution.

2. — o — There is wind beneath the couch.
   Confusion.

Magicians and exorcists are called in.
Auspicious.
No mistakes.

The conflicts within you arise from obscure, esoteric forces. To find a resolution to your problems consult those who deal with such forces: yogis, psychiatrists, astrologers, parapsychologists, etc.

3. —o— Only strong gusts of wind
beating against the house
can penetrate it.
You will regret it.

Although your way is to remain in the background, do not hesitate to act whenever the situation calls for action. If you hesitate you will become embroiled in binding confusion and action will become impossible. Your inability to act will be obvious. Others will take advantage of you.

4. —x— The hunter takes game
for its threefold use.
Guilt disappears.

The hunter nourishes himself; he loves and respects his prey; he is without pride and he communes with God as he gives thanks for his success. Like this hunter, you make full use of your resources, considering equally your material life, emotional life, and spiritual life (artha, kama, and moksha). You are able to find some good in everything.

5. —o— *Auspicious*
if you keep to your course.
There may have been a bad beginning,
but there will be a good ending.
For three days before you make any changes
consider them carefully;
for three days after you make any changes
reconsider them.
Advance.
Guilt disappears.

You must somewhat modify the reticence prescribed by the oracle of this hexagram. Your situation is bad. It must be changed. You are the only one who can change it. Now is the time for a fresh start. But you must carefully consider the changes you wish to make. They must be contemplated for a while in a modest and peaceful state of mind. Once you have initiated the change in your situation, you must remain alert to the possibility that it will not work. If, in practice, your attempt at reform does not live up to your expectations be prepared to chuck it in and begin again. Identify what needs changing in your life. Plan the changes well. Do not be afraid of backtracking.

6. —o— The wind dies under the couch.
    It no longer has the power to penetrate the
    crevice by which it entered.
    Ominous
    if you keep to your course.

Your quiet reticence has brought you face to face with evil. React. Draw back. Leave it. Do not try to influence it. Beware!

58

Twee · Pleasure

The Marsh below	The Marsh above

O R A C L E

The surface of the marsh is still;
the inner marsh seethes with life,
Beside it friends sit and talk,
The conversation is easy
but the communication between them is deep.

*Success
if you keep to your course.*

I N T E R P R E T A T I O N

A r t h a ▪ Every experience gives you pleasure. You are always content. Your quiet, untroubled character is open and accepting. You see no reason to defend or disguise your deepest feelings. Your imperturbable ingenuousness gives solace and hope to others. You give others the opportunity to reveal their deepest feelings, to share in your sense of pleasure.

K a m a ▪ The image of the oracle says it all. Quiet and content with each other, you and Friend share the deepest, most persistent communication, unexpressed, and unencumbered by selfish needs or competitive egos.

M o k s h a ▪ In the balanced flux of the universe even pleasure has a dark aspect. Your capacity for pleasure could deflect your spiritual course. Do not let pleasure pass for enlightenment. This danger can be avoided by keeping in touch with the serious, searching sides of your closest friends. Remain open to those quiet revelations of deep conversation that make lasting, intimate impressions. In the spirit of this hexagram, a most pleasant way to avoid danger.

L I N E S

1. —◦— The pleasure of inner peace.
   Auspicious.

Your capacity for pleasure arises from your saintly lack of desire. Nothing tantalizes you, nothing compels you, nothing disappoints you—everything pleases you.

2. —◦— The pleasure of sincerity.
   Auspicious
   but do not look back.

While you enjoy your pleasure, do not act in any way that might embarrass or discourage others.

3. —×— Indulging in pleasure.
   Ominous.

Your pleasure does not arise from a total enjoyment of all experience. It is limited to mindless delight in the sensual world only. Your life is a spiritual vacuum that attracts sensual pleasure—pleasure that serves to blind you to your true emptiness, pleasure that protects you from despair.

4. —◦— Anticipating pleasure.
   Auspicious,
   but be cautious.

Do not weigh one pleasure against another. When all things are pleasurable, all pleasures are equal. You must come to realize that you cannot make a mistake. There are no mistakes.

5. ——o—— Misplaced trust.
   Beware!

Pleasure makes you generous, friendly, sincere, and trustful. It also makes you vulnerable to people with opposing principles. Danger! You may feel pleasure in their company. But you are under no obligation to associate with them. You can break off in a gentle and inoffensive way.

6. ——x—— Enticing to pleasure.

You are caught up in pleasure. You have no direction other than experiencing pleasure. You are so involved with pleasure that you have dulled your positive feelings as well as overcome your negative ones. Taking pleasure is so habitual that you no longer enjoy it. No true pleasure.

59

Hwen ▪ Dispersion

*The Deep
below*

*The Wind
above*

O R A C L E

The air moves above the water;
the water evaporates.
The ancient kings were pious
and dedicated themselves to serving God.
They built the temple;
the present king worships there.

*Success.
Keep to your course.
You may cross the great water.*

I N T E R P R E T A T I O N

N o t e ▪ All situations and problems in the practice of artha
and kama are only egotistical fantasies and anxieties; even the
practice of moksha—which would include the casting of the I
Ching—depends on the existence of a certain amount of egotism,
a certain amount of self-consciousness that ultimately is false,
illusionary. You are fortunate—if you move with this hexagram—in being able to resolve your difficulties, solve your
problems, by ridding yourself of the entire egotistical, self-
centered mechanism that projects them. This is a hexagram of
perspective. You are within reach of realizing your existence as a

moving instant in a changing universe, of seeing your true place in the rhythm of life and death and in the patterns of men and society.

A r t h a ▪ This is the hexagram of charity: charity given or charity received—depending on which side of the tracks you are on. Aware of the illusionary nature of the concept of possession, you give to others whatever you do not use. Or: aware of the illusionary nature of the value of possession, you receive what others give you without shame and without feelings of debasement. Your practice of artha, your day-to-day life, interests you only as an example of the warp and weft of the divine pattern. You have no selfish, egotistical interest in it. In the eyes of others this is regarded as the ultimate in daring and the ultimate in success, no matter what your position on the socioeconomic ladder.

K a m a ▪ This is the hexagram of free and uninhibited love for all. You are in an intense and lasting relationship—with everything; you love Friend passionately and faithfully—and Friend is everyone. You are envied by those whom you love.

M o k s h a ▪ This is the hexagram of the brief ego-destroying religious experience. Your way is the way of religious ecstasy attained through ritual. Your way is the experience of death and then a return to life. Your way is the ultimate, eternal union with the One and All, and then a falling back into the illusory wave of time and space—but now with an enlightened perspective gained by your acts of ecstatic devotion.

L I N E S

1. —×— Rescue
        with the help of a strong horse.
        Auspicious.

If you act soon, your selfless, unconcerned perspective can be beneficial to others involved in the situation.

2. —•— Things fall apart;
          he seeks shelter.
          Guilt disappears.

To gain your selfless, unconcerned perspective you must pass through certain disagreeable stages: snobbishness; scorn for people who retain their illusions; even frustrated anger at what seems the pigheaded blindness of those close to you. But these stages will quickly pass. You have broken through the hypocritical facade. Your illusions have disappeared like the emperor's new clothes. Now you stand naked, like the emperor. The next step is for you yourself to be revealed as an illusion.

3. —x— He no longer cares for his own self.
          Without guilt.

Because of your enlightened perspective in which you place no value on the "self," you do not take care of yourself. Since you possess an enlightened perspective, it is useless to say to you that by not taking care of yourself you do not follow the natural pattern of change in the universe. You know there is only one pattern and that is the pattern that is being followed. However, on examining the patterns of existence of most sentient and nonsentient beings, you must admit that not taking care of yourself is definitely one of the odder patterns.

4. —x— The man scatters all the factions.
          He is cleverer than most people.
          Now he can see who stands out.
          Auspicious.

You must temporarily suspend your involvement with friends and associates. From a distance—both in time and space—you will be better able objectively to examine them, their characters and principles. True friends will stand out. With them you will soon be able confidently to reestablish your contacts. The others will feel resentment or will be puzzled and hurt. Such feelings will not last for long.

5. ──●── The man sweats as he makes his pronouncements.
       He empties the royal granaries
       and disperses the grain abroad.
       No mistakes.

You are energetic in your efforts to help your fellow man. You are a whirlwind of generosity.

6. ──●── The man avoids bloody wounds,
       going until he is out of harm's way.
       No mistakes.

The spontaneity and impulsiveness that accompany your enlightened perspective will carry you to the edge of personal physical danger. A Buddha nature would move calmly ahead and be destroyed. If you retain or recall an iota of the illusion of self, you can easily, safely escape the danger. Saving yourself is not backsliding into egotism. Continue on your egoless way.

60

The Marsh
below

The Deep
above

O R A C L E

The lake within the deep.
The superior man is systematic;
he confers on points of principle.

Improvement;
but if the restraint
is severe and difficult
it will not last.

I N T E R P R E T A T I O N

A r t h a · You possess an unlimited diversity of interests.
You react to all events, no matter what, with an uninhibited
responsiveness. It would seem as if you have achieved perfect
personal freedom. But your totally indiscriminate bevy of multi-
farious interests and activities affords you all the freedom of an
astronaut adrift. You are not an amorphous vacuum for experience; you are a human being with individual tastes, needs, capabilities; an individual personality and character. You cannot
contain all human potential any more than one lake can contain
all the water in the world. You will be truly free only when you
fully understand your personal limitations—what you want to
do, should do, can do; what you do not want to do, should not do,
and cannot do—and live within them. Danger: do not carry this
advice too far. Beware of arresting untried personal potential.

K a m a ▪ You have in your mind an image of yourself as "the ideal lover," who can be all things to Friend. Your part in your relationship with Friend is a constant striving to live up to this ideal. But this impossible ideal is a mass-media myth. It has little to do with your true self. Look at yourself realistically. Taking into account your individual personality, with its own special limitations, you can discover how to be a perfect lover realistically, on your own terms. You will have to eradicate whatever conventional lover's mannerisms are inimical to your true self. These will be replaced by more honest and sincere and more personal ways of expressing your affection.

M o k s h a ▪ There are an infinite number of paths up the mountain—but every man can take only one. Do not be a spiritual dilettante. Discover which way is your way, which way is most sympathetic and comprehensible to you—and stay with it. Your openness to spiritual influences from all sides has led you on an erratic horizontal path. Limit yourself to a single, fitting spiritual system and discover the expansive and direct road to the top.

L I N E S

1. ──◦── He will not leave his own hallway.
   No mistakes.

Take no action. Wait until it is perfectly clear exactly what action you should take.

2. ──◦── He will not leave his own courtyard.
   Ominous.

The time for action has come. Act immediately, without delay— now. Anxious hesitation will bring disaster.

3. ──×── The man is without restraint.
   Eventually he will lament.
   And there will be no one to blame
   but himself.

An extravagant life based on principles of pleasure leads to unhappiness. You blame the libertarian, amoral culture for enticing you to excesses. But you are a free agent; the fault rests entirely with yourself. Recognizing one's own limits is especially important for a hedonist such as yourself.

4. — x — Quietly and naturally
            he observes the proper restraint.
            Success.

The restraints you set on yourself must be realistic. If they are too strict, your life will be a constant struggle to live within them. If they are too lenient, your life will be filled with indecision, worry, and regret. Your restraints should fit you naturally and easily, be neither too severe nor too lax. They should not inhibit your proper activities. In fact, you should not notice them at all.

5. — o — His restraints are easy to bear.
            Auspicious.
            Honor
            if you advance.

You have a responsibility to set restraints on others. You manage to fit the restraints perfectly to the requirements of the situation while infringing as little as possible on the freedom of others. This success will bring honor and advancement.

6. — x — His restraints are difficult to bear.
            Ominous
            if you keep to your course.
            Guilt,
            which eventually disappears.

You have a responsibility to set restraints on others. The restraints that are required infringe cruelly on the freedom of others. You feel a sense of guilt about the unhappiness you cause. After a time, you will see that you only did what was necessary.

61

Khung-Fih  · Understanding

The Marsh
below

The Wind
above

O R A C L E

Wind blows across the marsh.
The superior man weighs
all litigation carefully,
and stays all executions.

Pigs and fishes.
Auspicious.
Keep to your course.
You may cross the great water.

I N T E R P R E T A T I O N

A r t h a ▪ Your greatest strength lies in your clear vision.
You view the world without prejudice, with an uncluttered,
healthy mind. You deal with people humanely, unselfishly,
lovingly. You understand yourself and can empathize with everyone, even those who feel antipathetic or hostile to you. The bond
between you and your fellow men goes beyond cultural differences. It is not simply a sympathetic similarity of hopes and
fears. You sense the divine image in all men and you perceive the
tragedy of the human condition. The close attachment you feel to
your fellow man is not forced. You cannot control it. You cannot
turn it off or on. You may even not be completely aware of it, as
such. According to the values of your culture you are not an

extraordinary person. But anything you undertake will be successful. The time is right for far-reaching changes and momentous activity on your part.

K a m a ▪ You are fortunate that you can love Friend as much as you love others not as close to you. This is not as cryptic as it sounds. Most people can find it in themselves to love mankind in general with a humane and unselfish love and to treat acquaintances with warmth and fairness; but many of the same people find it impossible to love those close to them without anxiety and to treat them as brotherly equals. What you may lack in the romantic graces or the popular affectations of affection, you make up many times over by the health, warmth, and humanity of your love for Friend.

M o k s h a ▪ You are not a saint. A saint, a bodhisattva, is one who has been enlightened and returns to live in the world according to his revelation. You have no need for enlightenment because you have not yet lost the self-knowledge that most people lose at an early age. A revelation is only the conceptualization of what you have understood all along, naturally, instinctively, and thoughtlessly, without revelation. Spiritual practice, the practice of moksha, for most people is like a journey from darkness into light. For you it is a simplehearted and—yes—simpleminded celebration of your constant, always unenacted, unconceptualized, union with God.

L I N E S

1. ——o—— The man rests in himself.
    If he were to seek outside of himself
    he could not rest.
    Auspicious.

You appear to act fairly and unselfishly toward everyone. But your deep reactions to others are not fair, not selfless. You judge them on the grounds of secret knowledge. You evaluate them in terms of secret goals. Your friends are not aware of the real basis for your relationships. This is the line of the master spy, the skilled adulterer, the clandestine satanist.

2. ──o── The crane among the reeds calls
   and her young respond.
   "I have some delicious morsels here."
   "We'll share them with you."

This indicates a joyous and meaningful relationship with a member of the same sex—possibly, but not necessarily, sexual.

3. ──x── The man meets his mate.
   Now he beats the drum. Now he stops.
   Now he weeps. Now he sings.

Your everyday fulfillment, your passing joys, completely depend on your relationship with someone else. If things go well between the two of you, you are ecstatic; if things go badly, you are miserable. Outside of this relationship you can find no cause for either satisfaction or disappointment. Without other elements in your life to modify your feelings, you are continually buffeted between the extremes of joy and sorrow. You are totally involved in the maya of romantic love. Do not let an unromantic era impose a negative self-evaluation of your way of being. If you feel fulfilled by this all-involving, ego-consuming Tao, do not let the cynicism of sophisticated onlookers cast a pall over it.

4. ──x── The moon is nearly full.
   Only one horse breaks his traces;
   one horse remains.
   No mistakes.

A friend has suddenly turned away from you. The relationship is crumbling. You are not responsible. You have no power to change it.

5. ──o── The man possesses self-knowledge
   and joins closely with others.
   No mistakes.

Your natural, uninhibited and indiscriminate affection and sympathy for others without exception has drawn together—through you—many people basically dissimilar, even antipathetic, to each other. As long as you are around you bring everyone together with your example of a generous, unprejudiced spirit. If, for one reason or another, you withdraw from the situation, all hell may break loose. This is unfortunate, but you are in no way responsible for the selfish attitudes which make men enemies of one another.

6. —o— Chanticleer mounts to heaven.
  Ominous.

You have a verbal gift. You easily convince others of your heartfelt warmth and sympathy. Do not talk so much. Let your daily life, your way of being, speak for itself. Stop touting yourself.

62

Zhaou-Kwo · Smallness
in Excess

The Mountain
below

Thunder
above

O R A C L E

Thunder high on the mountain.
The superior man is judicious in his conduct;
in a time of modesty, he is especially reserved;
in a time of mourning, he is especially sad;
in a time of economy, he is especially frugal.

Improvement.
Keep to your course.
Take on small tasks
and shy away from large ones.
Listen to the skylark
who sings most sweetly as he begins his descent.
Very auspicious.

I N T E R P R E T A T I O N

A r t h a ▪ The skylark is a creature of the earth—frail
clay; on the wing, he is only a sojourner in heaven. Even when
soaring, the skylark belongs to the earth, relates to the earth,
and seeks his sanctuary there. You occupy an elevated social
position, hold certain honors, account for certain important responsibilities, or are in some other way favored . . . while, in fact,

you are not suited for the position at all. Since you are essentially inadequate for the role, and had no ambitions for it, you can be considered extremely fortunate, which accounts for the "very auspicious" oracle. Attempt no major undertakings. Do not try to take further advantage of your luck. You can be happy and successful in your minor attempts. Maintain common, everyday attitudes, as cautioned in the oracle. Express reserve when it is expected of you, not reform or philosophy; express sorrow when it is expected of you, not fatalism or piety; express frugality when it is expected of you, not extravagance or charity. Do not let the heights you inhabit dizzy you. Be yourself. Know who you are.

K a m a ▪ Friend's involvement in your relationship is much deeper than yours. The relationship is more important to Friend than it is to you. You mean more to Friend than Friend means to you. No stigma of unfairness or insensitivity attaches to this situation; you are both free individuals. Love is not a commercial bargain, obliging you to love as much as Friend. As long as you are free of false ideals and feelings of guilt your relationship with Friend will be happy. Know who you are and be it; know what you feel and express it. Your side of the relationship is low-key, not so emotional, more casual than Friend's—but Friend does not judge you and makes no demands on you. The potential danger for you is a tendency to feel you must equal Friend's ardor, that you must somehow soar to where Friend is, that you must return Friend's passion in kind. But Friend's love for you is love for you as you are. Synthetic emotions would cause confusion—Friend would no longer be sure of you; and conflict—Friend would resent the dishonesty.

M o k s h a ▪ You have a natural gift for transcendence. Like a medium, a reader, a healer, or a water diviner, you have the innate, untutored ability to make intimate, absolute connection with the One and All. There is something within you that leaps the limits of your mind and hurtles the boundary of your body, passing through the barrier of your karma. This is no achievement of yours—it is a gift. Outside of this gift, you are not at all involved with spiritual matters. You do not struggle to resolve paradoxes with revelations. You do not devote yourself to performing incessant rituals until their absurdity brings enlightenment. You have never even simply abandoned yourself to fate. Yet you are blessed with a beautiful and charitable spiritual voice that does not come from your understanding or pass through your consciousness. This is "very auspicious." But remember Cassandra. The danger: hubris, pride.

L   I   N   E   S

1. — x — The skylark flies too high.
   Ominous.

You are not prepared to maintain the position into which you have been placed. You are not prepared to meet the responsibilities that have fallen on you. You are not prepared to respect the honor that has come to you.

2. — x — The woman bypasses her father
   and meets her mother.
   The man bypasses the ruler
   and meets the minister.
   No mistakes.

You have been given an important responsibility—one which was unsought by you and for which you are unprepared. It has come to you not in the usual way, but through unusual channels, perhaps in the stress of an extraordinary event: in an emergency, for example, when your single qualification was that you were the most available person. Accept your good fortune and conscientiously do your best. Feel no guilt, for you have done no wrong.

3. — ⊙ — The man has taken no precautions;
   others take advantage of this.
   Ominous.

Your position causes resentment among those who cannot accept the whims of fate. You must be extremely careful. Because of your insufficiencies, you are prey for those who consciously would do you ill.

4. —●— The man successfully plays it by ear.
   Advance
   boldly, but with caution.

You are in conflict with someone else. Hold yourself back. Try to keep from getting involved. Be wary. Do not be aggressive. Do not be conciliatory. Stand as aloof and above it all as you can. Do not indulge yourself in anger, impatience, or despair.

5. —×— Heavy clouds from the west,
   but no rain.
   The prince shoots an arrow into the cave
   and hits a bird.

You expect good fortune at any moment. Many indications point to you as the recipient of impending honors. But you may be overlooked in favor of someone else better qualified to deal with the responsibilities that attend the honors you covet.

6. —×— The skylark flies too high.
   The man exceeds his limit.
   Self-destruction.
   Ominous.

This is the misfortune of Icarus. Inadequate in the first place, you have tried to take advantage of your fortunate position. Now things are completely out of your control and are going against you. This is the line of a downfall.

63

Khee-Tzhee ▪ Completion

The Sun
below

The Deep
above

O R A C L E

Water suspended above the fire.
The superior man considers the potential evil
and guards against it.

Success
in minor matters.
Keep to your course.
An auspicious beginning
may bring a disordered end.

I N T E R P R E T A T I O N

A r t h a ▪ The course of your life has been fulfilled. This hexagram represents the moment of completion, which is also the first moment of falling apart. Both the inevitable flux of the ancient Yin and Yang and the entropy theories of abstract physics acknowledge the impossibility of perfect harmony remaining inert and intact. You have been moving toward an ideal (the perfect future); you have just now attained it (the perfect present); from now on your movement will be *away* from the ideal (the perfect past). This moving away is unavoidable, at least in the realm of the concept of time. Enjoy your moment of peace and perfection now! Now, enjoy these subsequent moments of intruding chaos, without regret and without looking back. Be at peace within yourself although in conflict with outside elements. Do not value the glorious past over the difficult present or you may find you have become as brittle and immobile as Lot's wife. Don't look back!

K a m a ▪ Your relationship with Friend is in a time of harmony, a time of fitting together and being yourselves together—although not necessarily a time of emotional climax or a sensual peak. You are wholly at peace together. Although change makes deterioration of this balanced peace inevitable, it is not inevitable that you must suffer because of it. Although you cannot retain all the elements of your present idyllic situation, you *can* retain the assured, unselfish peace that comes from it, the peace you now experience. If you meet future dissension still at peace with each other, you cannot be harmed by it. Be like the two ends of a single board tossed by the sea.

M o k s h a ▪ An enlightened vision perceives time as flux, the flux of development and deterioration, creation and destruction. An enlightened mind conceives of time as an expression of the One and All: as Yin and Yang, the dance of Shiva, or death and resurrection. You can enjoy the beauty, balance, and justice of your own deterioration, nulling it. Now it is not deterioration; it is a function of the universe, God's inhaling. (At the moment of enlightenment there is no flux at all; only timelessness.)

L I N E S

1. ——o—— The man puts on the brakes.
   The fox wets his tail.
   No mistakes.

You have been swept off your feet by the progressive and avant-garde trends of the times. The principles that generate this burgeoning cultural movement are similar to your own personal principles—but they are not identical. Before getting carried away, examine your own principles and limit yourself by them. If you blindly, indiscriminately follow these fashionable ideas you must expect major disillusionments and inner conflicts whenever the popular culture diverges from your inner principles. If you follow your inner principles first, you can deal honestly with every eventuality, even if it means once in a while bucking the trend or setting off on an unfashionable course.

2. — x — The woman in the cottage
       has lost her window screen.
       Do not seek it.
       In seven days you will find it.

Things have been going so smoothly for everyone everywhere that your capabilities and your potential have gone unnoticed by others. Knowing that you actually have a valuable contribution to make, you have a tendency to try to impose yourself. But to present yourself to others who do not accept you is to lose yourself. You must be patient. In the inevitable flux of the world and its affairs, your time will come.

3. —o— Kau Tsung invaded hell's provinces
       and after three years subdued them.
       Smaller men should not involve themselves
       in such enterprises.

The successful fulfillment of one phase of your life has led you to identify with a historical, fictional, or mythological character who has, until now, represented an ideal for you. Identifying with this idealized hero may lead you to believe that you can undertake the same tasks as he, and set the same goals. An objective comparison between yourself and the fabled hero should apprise you of the foolishness of such a conceit.

4. — x — The man carries a store of rags
       in case his boat leaks.
       He is constantly watchful.

Although you have brought things to a successful conclusion, there are still certain dangers inherent in the situation. The boat may not leak when it is launched, but a boat *can* develop a leak at any time. You must provide yourself with the means to patch up your affairs if and when the need arises. But there is a point beyond which you can become too watchful, too much on your guard, so much so that you can no longer enjoy the pleasures and rewards that accompany the fulfillment you have achieved.

5. —o— For the spring sacrifice
the neighbor to the east slaughters an ox;
but this is not equal to
the small sacrifice of the neighbor to the west,
whose sincerity is more worthy of benediction.
Beware of being ostentatious.

6. —x— He is in over his head.
Peril.

Instead of looking back at your past success with regret and a sense of loss, as cautioned against in the "Artha" section above, you look back with self-admiration. Instead of just innocently glancing longingly over your shoulder, you have halted in your steps, turned completely around, and gaze in hypnotic rapture at your past glory. You must continue to move in your Tao or disaster will result.

64

Way-Tzhee ▪ Almost There

The Deep below

The Sun above

O R A C L E

Fire over the deep.
The superior man sees things as they are,
and gives each thing its allotted place.

It seems to the little fox
that he has crossed the stream;
then he gets his tail wet.
Success
if you are like the man.
Failure
if you are like the fox.

I N T E R P R E T A T I O N

N o t e ▪ This little fox crossing the stream is proverbial in China. If he goes a little too boldly and confidently—unlike a wiser, older fox—he is likely to get wet. At the very end of the crossing his over-confidence reaches its peak, he feels his feet on dry ground, he relaxes his vigilance and his tail drops into the water.

A r t h a ▪ You are trying to make sense out of a strange, unprecedented situation. You and the people involved with you are so disparate, so unsympathetic to each other, so out of touch with each other, that you must exist in a constant state of alertness and readiness. Whatever you do, you have no way of knowing what the reactions of others will be. Thus it is impossible for you to predict or direct the eventual consequences of your own actions. So far you have been lucky in the steps you have blindly—as it were—taken. But do not let your erstwhile success delude you into believing that you possess some sort of sixth sense for dealing with the inconsistent, chaotic elements in your life. Watch your step. You suddenly may find yourself embroiled in what you have been trying to avoid with so much effort.

K a m a ▪ The direction of the force of fire is upward. The direction of the force of water is downward. When the fire is *above* the water, as in this hexagram, they are unrelated and unreconcilable. Why are you and Friend together? You are so different from one another that it is impossible even to make comparisons or speak of contrasts. Examine the motives behind your attachment to Friend; it's likely they have nothing to do with Friend at all. If this is true, then there is no sense clinging to the relationship. However, there is a way that fire above water *can* create a unity. A fire can be built on ice—a bonfire for skating children, for example. In this case the antithetic fire and water are reconciled in the experience of the skaters. The water—as ice—provides a field for their activity; the fire provides the warmth, the energy, that enables them to continue. If you and Friend are part of a larger group—a religious order, a commune, or even just a family—your seemingly groundless relationship can play a fitting and meaningful role in the context of the larger group.

M o k s h a ▪ Elements of your activity are contrary to your spiritual sensibility and to your basic principles of responsibility and action. You feel that since these other elements of your life remain on "a lower plane" than the spiritual elements, you can accordingly lower your standards and principles. But no one practice has any value over another. Artha, kama, moksha are equal and entwined in your life. To reduce the quality of one reduces them all.

L I N E S

1. — x — The fox gets his tail wet.
     Guilt.

You are resolved to take a drastic step to end the confusion that reigns in your life. But a time of confusion is actually a time to hold back. Refrain from action until enough elements have been resolved for you to evaluate the situation.

2. — o — The man puts on the brakes.
     Auspicious
     if you keep to your course.

It is not yet time to act. Meanwhile, prepare. Although you are still biding your time, waiting for the right moment, your Tao should already be in the Tao of the coming action. When you do act, the act will be a natural outgrowth of all that went before.

3. — x — Almost there, the man proceeds too fast.
     Ominous.
     A time to cross the great water.

The time for action has arrived. But do not act. You have not had enough time to gather the resources necessary to carry out the action. Let this opportunity pass. Withdraw entirely from the situation. Take a completely new direction. Break with your old contacts. Enter a new sphere of activity.

4. — o — The man steels himself to endure in hell's
     provinces,
     confident that for three years
     he will reap great rewards.
     Auspicious
     if you keep to your course.
     Guilt disappears.

You must act now. Quell all misgivings. You are acting on your most basic principles. Your freedom as an individual hinges on the outcome of your action. Act now. Without doubt or hesitation, carry it through to the end.

5. — x — Sincerity and brilliance shine in the man.
       Auspicious.
       Without guilt
       if you keep to your course.

You understand the irrational elements of your life. You sympathize with those unsympathetic to you. You find order in the clashing discord of present events.

6. — o — The man celebrates his victory.
       The fox gets drunk at the celebration.
       Without guilt
       if you are like the man.
       Guilt
       if you are like the fox.

Your ability to achieve harmony in a chaotic situation (see the interpretation of line 5 above) has led you into a life of pleasurable social activity, relaxing with others in the warmth of uninhibited friendship. Good times are a natural outgrowth of well-being. Do not let them degenerate into activities contrary to the principles on which your well-being is based. Beware of foolish excesses.

A graduate of Columbia University, SAM REIFLER is a
student of Eastern philosophy and an integrater of
Eastern and Western thought. He has written fiction as
well as nonfiction and makes his home in upstate New
York.